All Men ARE Dogs

YOU Are the Dog Trainer

Rick Fort

Copyright © 2016 Rick Fort.

All rights reserved. No part(s) of this book may be reproduced, distributed or transmitted in any form, or by any means, or stored in a database or retrieval systems without prior expressed written permission of the author of this book.

ISBN: 978-1-5356-0094-1

For my loving daughters whom I hope will learn from this advice and grow up to be excellent trainers.

Contents

Preface 1
How to Retrain Your Already Trained Man 5
How to Train an Untrained Man 11
"ASS:" The First Crack 21
You Could Use Some Training Yourself 25
Faithful as You Want 31
I'm in Respect with You 37
Smart, Sexy, and Lonely 45
Digging for Gold 49
Signs That Your Man is Cheating 55
Designed for Cheating On 67
Es-E-Ex 73
True Identity 79
Just Friends 83
Comfortdiction 87

Preface

So you want to know how men think? You want to understand where your man is coming from and what games he may be playing? Well, I'm a man, and I'm spilling the beans. I'm telling you secrets that your MAN won't tell you. I'm telling you what women's magazines try to tell you and fail because many of those articles are not coming from a true man's point of view, but from a woman's point of view of a man's mind, or some psychologist who overanalyzes how men truly are. It does not take that much research to explain us. We are not that difficult. It doesn't take a survey of "We asked one hundred men and 70 percent answered this way or that way." A man doesn't have to ask another man. He just needs to be honest with himself. If a question doesn't fit his character, he can, at least, understand what perspective another man is coming from. We are as simple as the alphabet, but we can be used to form many words and sentences, depending on the user. First, let me make something clear. These are my opinions based on my personal experiences and observations. Many women have come to me asking for advice on "their" men, and I've seen and heard so much that now I am ready to share my advice with you, the reader, right now.

Let me first say that I started writing this information while married and in a not-so-happy relationship in the late 1990s. I started a brief website posting articles on this very topic, as well as writing anonymously for an online magazine. I soon began getting hate e-mails from boyfriends asking me to stop telling all the "man" secrets. They said that I was going against the "bro" code. Nevertheless, the female audience at the time could appreciate the intel and value of information I provided for them to either leave or begin counter reacting to their mis-trained dogs.

So instead of chapters per se, I am going to lay this all out to you in the form of topics. Each giving you some insight on how a man thinks and his perspective on relationships, sex, cheating, and more. You will soon gain an understanding of how his mind works and why there are struggles within him that you don't understand. Some are aimed for you to share with him, and some are aimed to assist you in dealing with his past trainings and self-taught habits.

Let me start with one of the most-referenced clichés that mostly every woman has said at one point in her life: "All men are dogs." Well, ladies, let me tell you the truth about that. All men ARE dogs, but YOU are the dog trainer. They all react based on how good the trainer is. Now I know you may be thinking that some men have already been trained and that you are stuck with the results of the terrible training. Well, unlike real dogs, men can be retrained to your taste, but it takes a strong, mature woman who will have to compromise a little training herself. If you think that I'm wrong about calling your man a dog, then continue having the type of relationship that you are having, the relationship that you are not truly satisfied in, and you will find yourself carrying all the weight in your relationship, which is very similar to a donkey carrying his master's load, while the master directs him where to go. If you feel like you have that weight on your back, then this book may just be what you need.

Now, based on the statement that "All Men Are Dogs," we already have three good topics to start off with:

How to retrain an already trained man.
How to train an untrained man.
You could use some training yourself.

Now I know that you may be tempted to jump around from one topic to another, in any order, searching for those that may directly relate to your life, but I assure you that most of these topics go hand and hand and they are ordered to emphasis certain traits of the different type of guys that are out there. Most of the topics are about "how men think," and others explore the "mind of a woman." Notice the term explore is used for the woman and not for the man. I used explore because I believe a woman's mind (her thinking) is much more complex than that of a man. Men are basic creatures and only require one thing to please them. No, not sex. Consistency. Women, however, are more complex and require top scientists, a host of daytime talk shows, soap operas, and novellas to explain them. I'll expound on this more throughout our session of topics, and you will soon see a nice picture of what I'm talking about. Just keep one thing in mind as you read this. The moment you start thinking, "if I were him, I would do this or that," or "I don't think he…" then stop. The first mistake women make is to try to think like a man. It cannot be done. You're too complex, and we are too simplex. Now let's get started with our first topic.

How to Retrain Your Already Trained Man

Have you ever said to yourself, "My man has changed?" He is so much more different now than when you were just dating. He isn't going out of his way to see you. He isn't calling you as much as he used to. He used to be politer, and now he can be mean sometimes. In the beginning, ladies, this man would open doors for you, cook for you, even wash and comb your hair. He would listen to you talk about your exciting days, bad days, and your sad days. But now, you see a change. He isn't acting like that anymore. You haven't seen that side of him in a while now. You sit and think to yourself or chat with your friends, "My man isn't like he was when we met anymore."

Well, ladies, you are right. He is different, and let me tell you why. You let him change. You made him change. Your training was going very well, but you gave up the reigns of the relationship too soon. He may have treated you like the queen that you are, or the princess you longed to be, but it all came to a screeching halt late one night. It was that night you stopped training him and he started training you.

See, ladies, in most relationships with women, you were the head of that relationship when the two of you first met. YOU were the one in control, because HE wanted YOU. HE did whatever HE could to try to make YOU fall for HIM. And let no man fool you, ladies. They all want you to fall in love with them. Not like, but love. They want you to stay in love with them no matter what happens. They may not want you to follow them like a shadow and be a total fool, but they do want you to be head over heels in love with them. They want you to miss them if ever that relationship is over. They want that because they don't want you to desire anyone else, but them. It's ok to fall in love, ladies, but you don't have to just throw yourself at him all at one time because that will run him away or run him into being his natural dog self. That will start the change in your man. He was attracted to who you were before you started treating him like your husband. You were a strong-minded, independent woman. When you started submitting to him like a wife while you were just a girlfriend, you lost some points in the respect category. Some men may not look at it like respect, and some don't even know that the reason that they are acting the way they are is because of that, but consciously or subconsciously, that's pretty much what it is.

You started giving him everything a wife would give to her husband. Not only did you give him the "prize," you kept giving him ribbons as well. To top it off, you started giving him the "prize" on a regular basis. What are the ribbons you may ask? Let's see; cooking for him all the time, instead of occasionally. Cleaning his apartment every time it gets dirty. After all, you ARE THERE most of the time now, right? You're ALWAYS reachable when he is looking for you. You gave him a key to your place? He can drop by just anytime of the day, huh, because you want him to know that he can trust you. That's what you would expect him to do to you in order for you to know he can trust you. Right? (Hmm, remember what I said about thinking like a man?) That ribbon list sure can get long, huh? We can even add to that a little oral sex, too. Yep, you pretty much cover every duty a wife would do for a husband, but in the form of a girlfriend. So what perks are in it for him to take it any further? You're already submissive. You're already loyal. You're already allowing him to make decisions for you, WITHOUT the RING.

So, now what do you do? I'll tell you. Put your feelings for him to the side and fall back in love with you. Stop depending on him or any man to be your hope and joy. That comes from a source that your man cannot provide. You will never receive the kind of love you want to receive, if you don't have that kind of love for yourself first. Don't sit and tell yourself, "I love myself," yet you let someone other than you treat you any kind of way. You can't give a man more love than you have for yourself, especially if he isn't your husband. And by love, I'm not just talking about butterflies in your stomach, birds singing around your head and all of that type of fantasy stuff. I'm talking about love as in RESPECT. Without respect in love, your love is merely a waste of your precious adult time. He must love you enough to respect you and you must love him to respect him. There is no compromise where you only show respect, and he treats you like an underprivileged puppy.

If you feel you must devote yourself to him because of a lack of self-esteem such as you thinking you are unattractive now and that he is your last salvation, you will never win him over. Deep inside, a man wants a woman who has pride and great self-esteem. If your man is the type that just wants you to feel ugly and that you must "have him" to make it in this world, then he isn't YOUR MAN anyway; he is your MASTER. I'm not going to tell you to leave him, but I will tell you this. From a spiritual perspective, you, as a woman, are to be his "helper," not his HELP! From any perspective, nobody should be put in a position in your life to constantly drag you down to the point where your self-esteem is being constantly put down. That's why it's important to love you first and build self-esteem before going into a relationship. Many women make the mistake of falling in love with a guy who always compliments them when no one else is. It makes you feel good to hear good things from someone else, doesn't it? Well, he knows it, too. If you don't believe it yourself, and if ever a time comes when those compliments stop, then your dependence on it from him will put your self-esteem at risk. Short and sweet, don't make your man your therapist.

Now, if you are in an abusive relationship, you really need HELP! And if you deny being abused by him and you really are, then 2 people are abusing you, him AND you. You are doing the bulk of it because you're sitting there taking it. There is NO EXCUSE for accepting a beating from the quote, unquote "man of your dreams." There is NO EXCUSE for accepting a beating from ANY man. If you two need to hit each other, then you don't need to be together. That goes for you, too. Just because you are a woman doesn't give you the right to hit that man. He can easily claim self-defense if you start waling at him because you're pissed off. Time and time again, women say a man shouldn't hit them, yet they start hitting him. If you want him to control his anger and not hit you, then you need to control yours, too. Neither should hit the other…EVER. If being abused is your dream, then you may choose to sign up with a pro-wrestling team and get paid for your services. If your spouse is abusing you, then you really need to seek professional help. Violence isn't the answer in any relationship. Again, if the two of you have to hit each other, then you don't need to be together in the first place. Don't try to work it out. Don't let him give you an excuse. Leave that relationship and don't let it grow further.

Ok, now that I got that out, let's get back to the subject. You need to get yourself back together the way you were when you met him. I don't mean go on a diet or lose weight or all that stuff (though, it wouldn't hurt to boast your ego), I mean how you were in your character. First, sit your man down and tell him how you feel. Tell him how you remember all those walks in the park, or all those times he used to say "I love you" and "I need you" and how you are the epitome of a woman. Those characteristics are still in him ladies; he just lost the drive to display them to you. Just tell him that, if he wants to continue ignoring and not pay attention to you the way he used to, then you just have to revert to not knowing him as good as you do now. And what do I mean by that?

TREAT HIM LIKE A STRANGER GIRL!

Treat him like you are back on that first date. Hold out, to hold on. Show him how you used to be. And I'm not just talking about sex either. I'm talking about everything. Yes, even if you now have kids involved.

Now don't get me wrong, I'm not telling you that you need to stop being a good, dependable woman in respect to the kids, or that you need to move out or break off the relationship. See, he has done it, and you are still together, and as a result, YOU are hoping, and wishing, and working on this thing alone. Still spend time with him "with" the kids. But let him know that quality time, such as dinners and movies need to get back into the picture. If he wants to be treated like a king, then you demand to be treated like a queen. If he really wants to take you out alone, without the children, then let him find a sitter or pay for the late night daycare. Not you, him. And if that is just not possible, let him sacrifice some time and take you out during the day before the children get out of school.

It really isn't your worry, how he arranges the time. Don't take ownership of that responsibility if the two of you are living together. Keep in mind that, when you were starting the relationship and that guy was interested in spending time with you, he always came up with these ideas and more in order for the two of you to get away. Don't put yourself in the position of having to figure out his schedule and what you are going to do with the children and all that, which he purposely puts into your lap. If he loves you enough, he will come up with a way. HE WILL. But you have to communicate to him what you are doing to resolve it and what you expect from him. I'm not saying bitch about it either. I'm saying be straight forward and talk to him. Be direct. Don't be long about it because you can only hold his attention for only so many minutes. But do talk to him. E-mail him. Write it in a letter if need be, but talk to him. Lay it out on the line that you are unhappy and that unhappiness is at an end as of right…NOW. Then show him how happy you are … without him. Don't walk around the house with an attitude afterward. Keep a smile on your face. Laugh a lot. But make yourself less available to his beck and call. Do not give in either. If he takes you out on one or two dates within a few weeks, that's not enough. You need to keep this up for a while. You need to be (and I'm making this word up) re-dated. He hasn't forgotten how either. He just doesn't do it with you.

If there are no children involved, then you are smooth sailing. There is no excuse for you not to have those dates, dinners, and quality time that you are wanting. If you are having problems with quality time and you and your mate do not have children, then you are better off single. I know there are times when you are a professional woman or he is a professional man where it's hard to schedule time together because of your hours conflicting. Also there are situations where both of you are in some type of higher learning institute were time is a factor. Nevertheless, let me remind you once again; when a guy is interested in a woman, HE WILL FIND TIME. Don't let him give you a lot of awesome excuses as to why he can't do it. Men are the authors of a good "reason why." He can give you the reasons why the sky is falling. He can give you reasons on his theory of the beginning of the universe and not know a single thing about science. Nevertheless, the beauty of a woman hypnotizes him, especially a woman of challenge. If you tap back into the source that you tapped into when you first met him, then you will see the many sacrifices that he will make to spend time with you. Tap back into yourself.

How to Train an Untrained Man

In most cases, during the beginning of a relationship, the woman is the head of the relationship. It is during that point in time that you have his undivided attention. You have control of something that he holds dear and selfishly. Desire! Right now, you are it. You are what he is thinking about when he is alone. You are what he is trying to get off his mind during those times in his daily routine that he needs to concentrate. As much as he tries, he fails. You are the breath of fresh air that he receives after a hard day's work or on those long days where everything went wrong. It was during that time that you had his attention, and you were sure that you had his attention. All you had to do was keep it.

Let me repeat myself again when I say that men are very basic creatures. It is how women see men or try to understand them that make them complex. Why? Because women think complex, thus making him more complex than what he really is. Now, "desire" is the driving factor that dictates every thought process that a man has from the time he says "hello", until the time he says, "I think we need more space." By the way, the phrase, "I think we need more space" is a statement adapted by men from women where it is now used as a way of really saying, "I need some time to spend with another desire I have, but I'm not quite sure how much time I need to fulfil that desire. Plus I don't want to realize later that I made a mistake by saying this to you, so I need to leave a window open in this current relationship in case I need to crawl back in that window, so saying it to you this way is giving you some kind of hope because I know that if you have hope that we are going to get back together, and I can easily talk my way back into your heart. So you go along now and wait on me, and be faithful to me while I go and do this one thing I really need to do, and if this other thing works out the way I want it to, I'll then let you know that it is permanently over." (Those were three long sentences because that's exactly how he thought it out or felt in his slick doggie kind of way.)

You must keep that desire going throughout the course of the relationship. It doesn't require a lot of extra time and planning in order for you to do that. It just takes some self-control on your part until you get that so-called man of your dreams. I would almost guarantee that most women that have been looking and looking and hoping and hoping and praying and praying for that perfect man, have actually met, turned down, passed up, or broke it off with him already. The perfect man for you, dear, is not someone that was designed specifically for you, but is specifically programmed by you. I know what you're saying, "I don't want a man that will do everything I want him to do all the time" And sometimes you say, "I want a man that will listen to me, understand me, take time out for me, communicate well with me, and trust me and I trust him." Well, you will usually find all of those things in most men in some way or form. He automatically displays it at the beginning of the relationship, but it will only last for as long as you keep the power on. Just like the clock on a VCR or stove. Once it's programmed, it shows the right time, but if there is a power surge where the power goes out, then that wrong time keeps flashing over and over again until you reset that time. Electronics need maintenance and cars need maintenance. In the same way, men are like electronics, and men are like cars, so let's just say that men need maintenance as well. Every now and then, you just have to reboot them.

Now before I continue with this, let me express a spiritual take on relationships for the godly woman who is also having problems looking for that godly man. Although I believe a woman is the head of the relationship in its beginning. I believe a man should eventually be the head of his household. But in order to be that head, he must know two things:

Number 1. That he also has a Head of himself, which should be his spiritual God. He must treat that relationship the same way he would want his Head to treat him. If he is not a spiritual man, and he believes or acts as if his world belongs to him where he directs his own morals and beliefs, then you may have a hard time trying to develop a 50/50 relationship with him. Of course, there are guys out there who are not spiritual and have a good since of decency, but the problem is, if you are spiritual and he is not, then there will always be a war going on in that household that rarely results in a peace treaty. For more information on that subject I suggest you read in addition to this, your spiritual guidance scriptures. (That would be whatever your religion holds as its bible.)

Number 2. Compassion. He must have some understanding on how women like to be treated and how to handle their submissiveness, as well as himself being submissive at the same time. If he can't handle those things, then you may want to reconsider him as spousal material until he gains experience in compassion 101. It has to make him feel good to know that you are feeling good. It has to make him feel sad to know when you are feeling sad. A man who has compassion will not go out on the town with the guys to have fun, if he knows you're at home lonely and depressed.

Generally, women don't want a man that they can always push around, where they can always tell him what to do and he does it. They prefer a man to stand up for himself with her and with anyone else. There's a since of security that a woman likes to have in a man. Most men believe this and, oftentimes, take it too far. They end up wanting to always be right and always trying to rule over her, thus lowering her self-esteem. Just because you can over power someone doesn't mean that you should practice that act. This brings us here to where you need to pick yourself back up and start retraining or training this untrained man.

I'm not suggesting that you try to change someone into what you want him to be. I'm explaining to you how to gain and keep the respect he should have for you. Remember the cliché "you can't teach an old dog new tricks"? Well, you can, however, get that dog to respect you where his old ways will not affect the way he is going to treat you in this relationship. You control how you want to be treated by the amount of respect he has for you.

In order to begin training a man who hasn't yet been trained, you must be mature enough to know that men and women think and reason a little differently than what other rumors may tell you. What you must realize is that you need to keep the respect that he currently has for you in tack. One way that you can do that is to not be in such a hurry to sleep with him. The average man thinks that, if he can sleep with you in a few days after he first meets you, then anybody can. Although he may try to pressure and push you into the sack, it will always be better for you to hold off. The longer you hold off, the more he will trust you in the future. Always remember that, when it comes to men, what you do in the early stages of the relationship will reflect the amount of respect and trust he will have for you in the future. Even if you say, "That just happened one time and that was with him," he will remember it and, later in the relationship, may show signs of insecurity and trust. If he has to put up with a big "Wall of China" just to sleep with you, then trust me, he will remember that wall when you just want to step out one night with your girlfriends. He will know that, if it took him a long time to sleep with you, then it will take someone else an even longer time, just to get your attention. In most cases, the earlier you give into sleeping with him, the less trust he will have in you in the future of that relationship.

So you want to know how long you should hold out from all the sexy want and drive you crave and the pestering you may hear from him, or the faking he may put on by saying, "Oh, baby, that's okay. I'll be ready when you are?" I'll tell you. More than six months. "DAMN! That's too long!" No, it isn't, and it wouldn't hurt to wait longer or even until you get married. That act of sex is the ultimate sacrifice you can share with him. In his mind, once he reaches that level of intimacy with you, there really is nothing else left. For you, it is marriage. For him, it is sex. Of course, marriage and children are a factor in his mind as the level of commitment he must make to you, but from the time he says "hello" to you, "What is your name?" "Can I call you?" "You are a very attractive woman," or whatever he may have said in the greeting stage, it has all been leading up to the moment that you have intercourse. That moment you took down that brick wall. That's the way he thinks. That's the way he is. You can't change that. Everything that he says, or may have said to you to make you believe that he was so sincere into admiring and learning so much more about you may not be a lie, but it is a cover-up for the desire to reach that moment. And when you give in to it too fast, as if it's just a form of holding hands, then you risk any respect that he will have for you in the future.

You have to understand something, ladies. For every one thing you give up in that relationship is a symbol of a brick in a wall being removed. The wall is your respect level that will be used from the day you first meet him to the date of your wedding (if it goes that far). When he gets your phone number…brick removed. When he holds your hand for the first time…brick removed. When he touches you on the shoulder… brick removed. When he kisses you on the cheek… brick… removed. When he gives you a hug and presses his chest against yours…brick removed. When he finally kisses you on the lips…brick removed. When he starts taking off your top… twenty bricks removed. The barrier is getting smaller and smaller and easier and easier to access, until he reaches that final and last brick to that wall. That final brick isn't a child. That final brick isn't marriage. Those are not bricks to him. That is called surrendering. The final brick is the act of having sex with you. Men surrender their lives when they decide to get married and have children. When a man decides to get married, he feels he is giving everything in his life up for you. It's not you breaking down a wall, but you winning a war, a war within him to continue to be the ruler of his world. Just as Christians teach you must surrender yourself to God, he must also surrender to you in order for you to get him married.

If he marries you after you get pregnant, then it isn't a true surrender; it's a trap. Although he may love you, he is now trapped into not making that decision on his own, but using an aid to assist him in making that decision. Trust me, ladies. You don't want that type of commitment from him. That doesn't come with respect. That gets you what you want, but not necessarily what he wants. You become his burden, not his desire. You must be his desire. Remain his desire, and he will gladly make you his desired burden and responsibility, where he feels loving you is his job and keeping you happy is his responsibility. He needs to see that and make you that for himself, not from you bitching it to him like, "You need to take care of your family. You need to be a real man." That's where you are going to lead yourself into needing the "How to Retrain Your Man" part of this book.

Earn your respect from him slowly. Most men who have been hurt before in a relationship usually have a vendetta to score against women. You have to end that, and not sleeping with him so fast is a good way to start. Also don't cheat on him. Don't break down. If you can take the temptation, you can do the kissing, rubbing, and holding thing, but no genital or naked hanky-panky. Just enough to let him know it's worth the wait. And when you finally reach the minimum six months… then… rock his world. When I say "rock his world," I mean don't just lay there and play stupid. Get into it and be a screamer and an overachiever. But… don't spend a night with him. And right after it is over, shower, get dressed, and leave. He must understand that, just because you went the distance, doesn't mean that you are now his property. Men will place a flag on some land quickly and claim it as being conquered quickly. Yes, he finally slept with you! Yes, it was good, like he thought it was going to be! But no he can't look at you as if he can sit back and relax because you are now soooo in love with him. What you do after that first sexual encounter is going to set the stage of how the rest of the relationship is going to go, and you are not ready to turn over the reigns just yet. This is going to leave him confused. And confused is exactly where you want him to be.

After the six months of waiting to have sex, don't sleep with him but a minimal of once a month or even two months for up to six additional months. Tease him but don't go through the act. You have to keep teasing him so that he knows you are interested in sex. You have to hold out to keep the respect and morals in tack. If he ever asks you about that long wait between sex acts, you have to tell him straight up, that the freak in you is saved for your husband when you're ready to become a bride.

Don't ever spend a night at his house until after a year. Yep, I said a year. If you find that too hard to do, then you are learning a lot about yourself as a woman, which is exactly why you should wait a year. What you learn about yourself is what most guys will try to figure out immediately. The better character you build for yourself, the more likely it would be for this man to give you the respect that you will definitely love when you're married. Don't bend either. Not even if he asks to marry you and give you the ring. Stay who you have presented yourself to be! Let who you learn to be through this become who you are. You can, then, be devoted to him AFTER the wedding. Failure to keep your respect in tack could easily lead to being engaged for years.

Don't let him come over in the middle of the night. Don't go over there in the middle of the night either. Don't ever let a man talk you into getting out of your home at three o'clock in the morning to drive over to his house and keep him company. That's ridiculous and completely insensitive of him to even ask you that. Remember, ladies, it's all about character. Whether he admits it or not, what you do and don't do will always come up later if you marry this man.

Now after waiting the six months, and if after all that time of him waiting to sleep with you, he lasts a long time before ejaculation, then be suspicious that he is sleeping with someone else. If he waited that long to make love to you, and it lasts over fifteen minutes AFTER insertion, then he is either sleeping with someone else or masturbating. After about two minutes, if he isn't ready to perform again, then you either wore him out, (hardly) or something fishy is going on. Don't misunderstand me, ladies. Guys can last longer than fifteen minutes. Not surprisingly over one hour after insertion. This isn't foreplay time I'm talking about. I said after insertion. If you make him wait for six months and he has had no sex whatsoever, don't EVEN expect a stallion in bed that night. At least, not the first go round. I know, I know, if you waited and he waited and you can go longer, so he should be able to, too, right? Not necessarily. With men, and as visual as we are, the longer he waits, the hornier and easier it is for him to pop off. It's like shaking a cola over and over again, then finally popping the cap. Yep, all over you, girl. You may feel slightly the same way, but most women naturally can last longer than a guy anyway. Even after you pop, you can still keep going for some time longer than most guys can.

Oh, and by the way, no oral stuff. Even if he does you, never do that until after you're, at least, engaged and ration both to him until you get married. If you just enjoy doing that, then wait, at least, a year before going there. Let him know you don't mind doing it, but it takes more than a verbal commitment to get you to do it.

Now I know you keep asking yourself, why am I so die hard about having you to wait for everything that you enjoy and you know that your supposed man enjoys too. Well in order to give you a better understanding of how many men think when it comes to marriage, let's start with another brief topic of discussion and then we will continue on with more training. Consider this… an intermission.

"ASS:" The First Crack

By far the oldest and most addictive drug that has conquered the world of man to date is the ass of a woman. As with other drugs, this drug, too, has a history that is proven to be reckless to many persons and lives, and it can affect an entire family. But unlike the other drugs that are haunting this world, professionals, scholars, and even the owners of this potent and additive drug have overlooked the ASS, and have failed to understand the addictive forces behind it, which has successfully made it a drug for most men. Because of this oversight, our culture has placed invalid morals on the substance that has resulted in a major turning point in our society. Yes, unlike their predecessors, women have put aside and rejected the user and admirer of this drug from utilizing it as he desires by placing limitations on its usages and its supply. Where, at one time, there was no limit to the stock piling of the drug, women in today's society have placed a limit of one ASS per household. This action created a chain effect that would revolutionize lives, families, and a rehabilitation program that would last a lifetime.

Now a typical male will, at any point and time, become totally distracted by the form of a beautiful ass, no matter where he is. It doesn't matter if he is married or unmarried, a professional, a bum, with a client, with his lady, in church, or in the hospital. This visual creature will not only look but also try to memorize its area and shape as if he will be able to duplicate it later in a lab. Oh, trust me. If it could be done, he would do it in a heartbeat. Even if he managed to glance and look away to show some type of dignity, the urge will overwhelm him where the thought of that awesome ass will haunt him for the next few minutes or, in some cases, the whole day. Rest assured that, somewhere during that day or the following days, one of his friends will know of the sight of the ass he encountered. It will be imprinted in his mind as if he saw a UFO. "Oh, man, you will not believe the ass on this lady I saw…" "Hey! The other day I was leaving the office and DAYUM, I saw this chick and…" "You will not believe this, but I saw the best-looking ass I've ever…"

An incident was recently shared with me of a female who was out drinking in this nightclub. Of course, this lady who shared this with me is packing a nice ass herself, and when she entered the club, every guy she passed attempted to stop her. After finally being able to sit down, this one particular guy approached her table and began chatting with her. Even after finding out that he was married, she still continued to chat with him. During her conversation with the man, he stated, "Me and my wife just had our first baby a few months ago. She is coming up here to the club in a few minutes, but she will be leaving right after that." He continued, "As soon as she is gone, would you like to go out for dinner?" Now, of course, his approach is shabby to begin with. However, the point here is how his whole character has been destroyed from the addiction that ASS has made on his life. With a wife, a new baby, and what should be a man feeling proud and excited about his new status in life as a father and a proud parent, this man is still out looking for ASS.

These actions are typically found in today's male. Now it's not because he doesn't want to be a proud parent or good husband because, more often than not, a man really does. But from a man's true perspective, one ASS just isn't enough to be happily married to. Of course, there are men who are married and feel happy and faithful about it, but it's because our society has told him he should be. If it were an option, he would certainly choose otherwise. Although one ASS will suffice, it's not a part of his chemical desires. The act of being in love with one woman may be a reality to him, but the desire of having more than one ASS around is embedded in his DNA. Being a faithful man to a woman takes a lot of hard work! If you are a woman and have been wondering why it's so hard for a man to commit to you, it's because he knows that marriage is a rehabilitation program. Just like a crack head needs to go to a clinic for help, every man shares his shoes for he, too, is a 'crack head,' except for him; it's the 'crack' of a woman.

You Could Use Some Training Yourself

THEY SAY THAT THE BEST way to a man's heart is through his stomach. Well, if you keep believing that, then you will find yourself alone and lonely. I haven't met a man yet who would choose a steak over some hot, perfectly planned sex. Yeah, yeah, yeah, sex isn't everything, but it is a big plus in keeping him interested. The best way to lose a man and push him out the door is to deprive him from expressing his sexual desires, even on those days that you are mad and angry and something has led him to the point of being in the dog house for the night. Continually putting him in that dog house is still depriving your man from those sexual desires. Let's also touch on any surprised acts of sex. Just as many women enjoy surprises, men like surprises also, and since it is a surprise, sometimes it's how you package that surprise that makes it even more interesting. I know you may have tried the old "put on a negligee" routine, and a lot of the times there were no sparks, right? Right. But have you noticed the reaction of your man when he sees a sexy woman on TV, in a magazine or even in a music video? Yes, that reaction that sometimes may cause you to become a little jealous or feel a little disrespected and earn him a side-eye or even a firm slap.

If you have hesitated on doing such acts to him because you may have gained a little low self-esteem because of your body, then be assured that it's not always your body that attracts a man but how you package your body. If you are within twenty pounds of the size you were when you first met him, then you are still in the "she is hot" range. Odds are that he is not tired of you; you just stopped playing with his fantasies. Ladies, if you've never danced for your man, dance. If you've never modeled for your man, model. You don't have to go and buy a new wardrobe if you can't afford it; you just need to improvise. Men like an erotic woman. She's not shy about being naughty. She's not shy about expressing or sampling the wild side of her personality. Now I know that there are some men out there that you think want you to always appear nice and conservative. However, no matter what you may think or what they may admit or say, they have had the fantasy of having a night with a sex goddess. Your job, dear, is to become that sex goddess. You need to find that fire that he may have failed to express or has hidden from you and become the fuel to make it blaze.

I know some of you think that you have gone the limits and tried "everything." But still he hasn't been giving you the attention that you need. We will address the other than "everything" limits in the "In Respect with You" topic later, but for the woman who has been too afraid to experiment, for the woman who has been too shy to please her husband, for the woman that has been more of a waitress and a maid in the relationship…for you, my dear, you need spice. You need to wake up and smell his pheromones. If you don't know how, it may be best if you stop reading how to magazines and use some other more visual aids to get in contact with his visual nature. The first place to look may just be the porn industry. Yep, I said it. PORN. As bad as that may sound to some, there are some women out there who could really use some of it to understand the kinds of crazy fantasies that some men think about. Not all men want to see it, but they all want to experience something from it. I would not advise you to necessarily try any of it to reenact, but to check out the look of the women, the look that many of the actresses have in their eyes. The lust they show for wanting their partner. It's not mainly the sex act that you need to observe, but the "how to appeal to a man" that you should learn. After all, as crazy as some of those films are, the fantasy of them comes from somewhere, and many come from the perverted mind of a male. The kind of mind you need to get in touch with that may have been hidden from you.

For example, let's talk about communication. Not about drama and not about how your day was but kinky communication. Try telling him straight out that you want him in your mouth right now. Try telling him that you want him to lick you immediately. Be naughty. Don't hint around with it. Just say it out of the blue. In a grocery store. In a movie theater. At a ball game. Just while driving or wherever just … SAY IT. Wherever you can think of saying something kinky like that, just do it. Then, actually do it! If you can't just then, don't let the day go by without actually doing it 'cause, if you tell him that on the phone and you don't follow through with it by the end of the day, then it's worth nothing to him and will possibly even piss him off. You don't want to end up falling asleep at 8:30 PM, and he's up pissed that you talked up a "good game." And now that you guys are finally home and the kids are all in bed, now your "good game" has gone to bed, too.

Keep the ideas flowing that will entice him to be comfortable in gaining your trust into his hidden sexual mind. Tell him to go with you for a short ride and take him to a twenty-four-hour newsstand or someplace where you can give him a magazine to hold and observe while you satisfy him. Try to come up with something outside of the house to give him the feeling of being sneaky and single and…naughty while giving him an awesome night to remember. Be erotic, ladies. Most men will love it. If he likes sports, give him a halftime break. Take a football or basketball or golf stick or hockey puck or soccer ball and strip naked and rub it all over your body for him. He will forget about that game and start his own super bowl. Improvise, ladies, improvise! The shy woman will be left lonely. If he even dares to ignore you, then masturbate right in front of him. Don't be offended. Close your eyes and masturbate right next to him. Even under a cover if you have to, but make sure he knows exactly what you are doing. And not by your nagging about it, but your moaning about it. You have to set the mood and not with an attitude. If he doesn't bite, then don't worry about it. Don't make a big deal about it. Finish yourself off and smile at him. Have fun with it. Be mature with it. You must stay confident with it.

Here's one, sew a nice necklace made of grapes and let him eat them from around your neck, chest, or bottom. What's even better is if you put them around him and eat them off him. Improvise, ladies, and give him the fantasies that he has been looking for on the Internet. You need to become his Internet. You need to become his video game console. You need to become his phone App. You need to concentrate on being his sexual playground.

All of these things are only if you've been in a serious relationship. This is not for the dater. Not for the new boyfriend you just met a few weeks ago or a couple of months ago. This is for a when you are in a serious, long relationship where the sparks seem to be going out. It could come to a point to where you may find yourself second to everything entertainment. Not the woman who is being cheated on, but the woman who has seen that spark leave that relationship and replaced with other entertainment in the relationship, whether in the house or outside the house, and you are not a part of it. This is the time to bring something back in the relationship, before he eventually runs into …well… her, the YOU that you aren't anymore but the woman that you became.

Let's focus now on the career woman who is totally dedicated to the job but who also has a husband. This can work out wonderfully for some couples, yet for others, it can be a nightmare. It sometimes may start off perfectly fine, but after some time or even years of it, your man can eventually feel neglected. It could come completely out of the blue for you, and you may be confused at first as to why he is all of a sudden acting as if he doesn't understand your schedule or as if he hasn't been a part of this growing career of yours. But, it happened, and now you are in it, and you see or hopefully have not failed to realize that he constantly complains about the amount of time your job takes up.

Face it, ladies. In a serious relationship, men want the same thing you want — to be number one. You don't want to settle for second place and neither does your man. Have you ever found yourself in a conversation or argument with your man about how you always delay doing anything that he asks you to do, yet you do whatever you're asked to do immediately for your job and business? Do you always have time for your job and barely find any time to spend with your man? An e-mail comes in and you rush to read it and immediately respond. This goes on at any time, day or night, but you aren't on call day or night for him. You have placed yourself into being a workaholic over being a wife-aholic. Sure, some instances of this behavior can be considered signs that you may be cheating on your mate with a lover, but I'm specifically speaking on the instances where the only instance of being cheated on concerns the cheating of your time and your commitment to your partner. This can be just as dangerous in a relationship as an outside love affair.

The answer in solving this issue sounds simpler than it really is. It will take a lot of understanding and consideration from you, as well as some sacrifices that you have to make on the career front. If you want a successful career AND a successful relationship, you need to become a master of work-life balance. "Work-Life Balance" should be your daily anthem.

This is where you don't give up your entire life for your career in place of life outside of your career. You have to find a balance, and the longer you wait to find that balance, the longer that relationship will suffer, and it can get very close to the point of no return. Your spouse is only going to sacrifice faithfully for so long. He will not ever settle for being number two, no matter how hard he may try to act like he is.

Put yourself in his position. If he works for a woman in a demanding career where he is always on the phone with his boss or someone at the company or answering calls and texts at any time, day or night; yet days, weeks, or months can go by without him fixing that broken door knob or fence or whatever household chore you've asked him to fix, then you will soon become uneasy. Yes, you can do it yourself, but that isn't the principle. You asked him to do it. You soon find this pattern in other situations where you ask him to do something, and it's always placed on the back burner, yet he constantly comes home and talks about his job and all the respect he is getting. You're finding that 80 percent of his conversations are job-related. He's constantly checking his e-mails, awaiting a new task to do or to stay in the loop on what's going on at the office, yet missing out on all the backed up tasks going on at home. Put yourself in those shoes, ladies, and you will find yourself eventually thinking about the famous woman's intuition. An intuition that men also have.

Faithful as You Want

He tries so hard to be the man that you want him to be, the man that he wants to be, the man that he has vowed to be, and the man that he knows he should be. There is nothing more that he would like to be than to be what he vowed to himself to remain. But no matter how hard he tries, if life deals out the right cards at the right time, in the right place, and with the right self-justifiable reason, a man IS going to cheat, if home isn't what home is really supposed to be. Now this isn't addressing the man that has never been faithful at any point in his life. It's not about the man that has been playing women all his life and has decided to get married because he just feels it's time to settle down. That style of man will more than likely find any excuse to mess around on his lady. No. This is about the true men out there who have really desired to get with a woman, keep that woman, and give his all to that woman. A man that is really into that "ideal family" lifestyle.

Yes, ladies, there are actually men out there who want to have a serious monogamist relationship. The fun and games are over in this man's life. His new party pleasure is settling down and starting a family. These types of men try hard to make a relationship work, but many of these men are usually married or in a very serious relationship with some of the worst women on the planet. Now what do I mean by "worst women" in that statement? I'm referring to the woman who portraits herself as to be a dedicated one-man woman. What did I just say? Yes, her. The woman that has painted a portrait of herself as the perfect example of a dedicated wife. She can go on and on and on about how she does this and that around the house and how his life is a life of comfort because she spends so much time taking care of the house or household needs. Yes, her. I'm not surprisingly talking about the woman that has flirted or even slept around with the mailman or had a little hanky-panky on the side while her husband was trying to put bread on the table. Those types of women are plentiful and always wondering where all the good men are later in life after they end up divorced. It's the little sweet one that was raised to take care of the household who, however, ends up neglecting the needs and desires of her man. Yes, of course, she will take care of the house, and she may make a very good mother. Yes, of course, she has a hint of independence (in her conversation when she shares her dreams about all she wanted to accomplish in life but never attempts to do so) and lists of "I don't do this" and "I don't do that like other women." Yes, of course, she is true to her word when she says she never messed around on a man before or how she was raised with good standards and morals. He loves those qualities which he sees in her from time to time and finds comfort in appreciating that. Women such as her would make the ideal wife if only she lived on her own before or ever stood on her own two feet for several years. However, usually this type of woman that I am referring to got married right after moving out of her parents' home and ended up being a stay-at-home wife and/or mom. What is missing in this picture is that she, oftentimes, has no clue as to how a man likes to be treated. She's been engulfed all her life in the role of the stereotypical stay-at-home wife.

This woman has been so sheltered from what the world is really all about and what people really desire, that she really believes that men want and need the exact same thing that many women want and need — conversation, companionship, and children. Those three Cs have absolutely nothing to do with what a man really expects in a relationship. He may have a desire for those things at some point, but they are not priority requirements.

What most men are more interested in is not what your girlfriends can teach you, but it's from what an honest man can share with you. A girlfriend CANNOT give a man's point of view. They can only advise you as to what they have gone through after they have concluded it to be a reality to them.

Men are basic creatures. There is no deep science to it, even though women's magazines have written special editions to define us. It doesn't take a psychological journal of 300-plus pages to describe us. It doesn't involve astrology, tarot cards, or a fortuneteller. All it takes to satisfy a man can be summed up in one word — consistency. Yes, I've already stated this before, and I will be restating it again as well.

Watch him and learn. He WILL NEVER CHANGE. I'm not talking about what you call his bad habits. I'm talking about his daily routine. Once you see what he likes and dislikes, from there, my friend, it's all about timing. Notice how better of a mood he will be in if you would let him wind down for about an hour after he gets home from work without you telling him every single thought you have thought all day as soon as he walks in the door. Let him create a routine for himself, and you will see a major change in your relationship. If ever you alter your man's routine, then you are risking the decline of his faithfulness.

"Routine? But the routine will not include me. Why should I let him be selfish and only think of himself?" you ask. That's not the routine I'm talking about. I'm talking about a routine that would allow him to have some quiet time (say thirty minutes of quiet time after coming home from work) and a routine that would enable him to fulfill his sexual desires with you on a consistent basis. You need to be consistent on how you please him, so much that he wouldn't have a desire to even masturbate. And a note to all the readers out there who like to use sex as a weapon: holding out on sex will not work to change this man. His God-given ego is not going to let you boycott his God-given desire. A popular statement says "A woman's glory is her hair," and in that same belief, I say, "A man's glory is a woman." You set the stage of all things him. If you aren't that stage for him, then there is an opening in his life. I'm a firm believer that a woman runs a relationship but most times gives up those reins and forgets how much power she actually has.

So simply put. If you are consistent at making love to your man, then he will consistently be faithful to you. If you are out of order for your monthly visitation, then you need to improvise a backup plan. A woman who is involved with her man's sexual interests will more likely than not have to ever worry about him going outside the relationship. So if that means watching sexual videos with him, then you need to get to watching. Don't feel threatened by the sexual content. You WILL learn something from the experience. If you ever caught your man masturbating, then it should have been your hand he was using. It is your total responsibility to keep your man sexually satisfied, and it's his to keep you sexually satisfied as well. If you are not getting satisfied, ladies, you need to tell your man what you think will get you there. It's total communication on every single level to make that relationship work.

Now I'm not saying that sex is all that a man wants, but I assure you that it's one of the main reasons that men cheat on women. It's either the lack of sex, or the lack of spice in the relationship. Now, on the other hand, when it comes to women cheating, men are lacking in what could be a barrage of items. It's usually not as much as a sexual reason for a woman to go outside a relationship, but a lack of time or even a financial reason. Women will mess around eventually when that loneliness that a man has forced upon her occurs. Her intentions are not to mess around but to just have someone to talk to or keep her company when her man is not there for her. Women need time and attention. The money that he may give and think will suffice her in place of his time will soon get boring. A money hungry woman will disagree with that statement, but it will eventually hit home for her when she is really in that position. The average male will believe that there is a substitute for time with something else. He figures that, if your time is occupied with something else (not someone else), then all is gravy. If he doesn't have money to give and he is not substituting something else with the time that he knows he should give you, then he gets paranoid.

Ladies, when your man is giving you a hard time about going out and having male friends, it is not you mainly that a man doesn't trust; instead, it's the other men that a man doesn't trust. Men know when they are not fulfilling something in a relationship. They just really think that they have time to make up for it later. Additionally, he knows that another man is going to point out the things that he isn't doing for you, because I guarantee you that the other male friend of yours is more than likely trying to get with you, as I've discussed in another topic.

Men, if you want your woman to be faithful, you have to spend time with your woman. You have to stop trying to make her fit into your schedule when you are not fitting into hers. You are going to have to listen to her, even if you don't feel like hearing her talk about what you consider "nothing" for an hour or more. You've had experience in that already before. Remember, when you first met her? Yes, you could listen to her talk all day. And now that you are tired of listening to it, you will, in fact, listen to the same from another woman. Don't! Take that same time and energy, and recycle it back into your own relationship.

If the both of you will compromise a little selfishness, then you should be on your way to a better understanding of what commitment is all about. These few notes of mine combined with a little common sense, respect, biblical principles, and your trusting in one another will only make your relationship better.

Now I know I have crossed several other areas on this topic that I'm sure you have experienced in your life. Those others areas will be addressed in other topics throughout this book. The primary focus you should keep here is how to keep your man faithful. Apply these rules after you have done your job at training your man. These methods we covered in the topic will keep him trained and pretty much so worn out, that he won't have the strength to step out of the relationship. But you need to keep your focus when doing this. You don't want your man to start ignoring you when you allow him to develop that routine that he needs.

If you are having problems with your man respecting you, then it's not yet time for you to apply this. You must train him to treat you right and then show him the rewards of doing so. I know a lot of women out there may have a problem with using the word train as it pertains to a man. Some say they don't have time for these types of games. Some say he is a grown-ass man and he should know by now what he needs to do in a relationship. Yes, all good points but believe this as well. Someone, if not you, is doing that training. Someone, if not you, is showing him the requirements to get with them or keep them interested. For you, I'm calling it "training him." The direct translation is "making him fall in respect with you."

I'm in Respect with You

"I love you." "He loves me." "I'm in love with you." "We fell in love." "I'm in Respect with you." I'm in Respect with you?

Of course, you will never directly hear, "I'm in respect with you," coming from a man. But those are the words that you need to hear. Those are the words you need to see. Those are the words that should make your heart go pitter-patter. Not "I love you." "I love you" has a lot of meanings, but many women long to hear that from a man. Those that have heard it usually hear it mostly in the early stages of the relationship, and the words fade away or get lost during the term of the relationship. Many movies and television sitcoms, portray men as afraid to say "I love you," but women in the real world hear those words so much that it's hard to determine if a guy really means it or not. Of course, everyone loves to hear, "I love you," but the word love is used so much now that you never really know when someone is sincere or just telling you what you want to hear. Is there really love anymore? Do people really fall in love anymore? Do men want to really be IN LOVE. Love, love, love. That four-letter word that keeps women in relationships that are not working out and may never work out. That simple four-letter word keeps many woman in situations where they suffer abuse, neglect and many nights of heartache. The same word that brings tears of joy also brings pain and agony.

But we keep falling into it. We keep looking for it. And many times we think we have found it, but it becomes lost again. So is it possible to keep what you have found? Is it possible to lock up the first moment that love is realized? When men say "I love you," are they being sincere? Does it even matter if they are sincere? Ladies, put your minds to rest. Start fighting that urge of wanting to hear that word from a man. Don't put all your eggs in that phrase because that phrase affects you ladies in ways that will lead you into thinking that he is sincere, even when he is not. What you really need before he falls in love with you is for him to fall in respect with you. If the words, "I love you" aren't displayed in him respecting you, then that love is totally irrelevant.

Here is an eye opener for you. When a man really falls in love with a woman, he falls in "respect" with that woman. What? What does that mean? It means that most men need to respect you first and love you second. If he respects you, then loves you, he will adore you. He will cherish you. He will not stop treating you like the queen that he started treating you like in the beginning. When a man says, "I love you," it can mean so many things that he can't interpret it himself. Most men don't know the difference between "I love you" and "I desire you." He can want you so bad that his mind feels like he is in love with you. But after he has had you…he starts regretting the fact that he ever told you that. In fact, he wants to just leave and do something else. I'm telling you, ladies, at the time he says "I love you," he really means it. But after that veil has been lifted from his eyes, and he sees your beautiful naked body or the intimate touch of your breast, and that warmth of your glory (aaaaaahhhhhhhhhhhhh) … it all goes away, only to return a few days later when he is reminiscing about that moment.

In most relationships, women make the man fall in love with his interest in her. He falls in love with her character and her body. You may have said to yourself, "I want a man to fall in love with not only my body, but my mind." Well, ladies, that's not good enough. Before you turn love over to him, you need to gain his respect first. Just because he says, "I do respect you," doesn't mean he does. You have to show him that you demand respect. Displaying how firmly you are grounded in your own self-worth will determine what amount of respect a man will have for you. Let me repeat that because it's very important that you completely understand that. I said, "Displaying how firmly you are grounded in your own self-worth will determine what amount of respect a man will have for you." You must, must, MUST show how much you respect yourself in front of this man. Based on that respect, his true love for you will remain and show in that relationship. When a man loses that respect, the love that he says he has for you is completely worthless. You don't want a man to just be with you because he has grown used to being with you. That happens a lot in relationships, where the feeling of love has left the building. Are you in that relationship? Has the feeling of love left and been replaced by routine?

A lot of times, couples remain together because of habit. They have gotten used to being together and the relationship is more of a habit than love. The "I can't wait to see her" feeling is gone. If you don't understand what that means, then I'm sure your man will understand. Ladies, don't become a habit. Don't become ONLY a routine for your man. You may say you want that, but let me tell you what happens to your man when your relationship becomes just another routine. Your man starts desiring a new show. Your man starts looking at life like cable TV, instead of the local channels that you are offering. He starts getting interested in things that both of you have never done, interested in things you say you will never do, things you are embarrassed to do or didn't think he would like. He starts remembering the fun he used to have in previous relationships, and pretty soon, he will start acting on that old school dream. That little respect that sprouted from the love that was planted first fades first, and the love will soon follow. All those little things that you did to try and gain his love will not be enough to hold your man's attention for long.

So how do you make a man respect you? How can you tell if a man has that respect for you that is equivalent to the love that you are searching for? Easy! By first respecting yourself. When that little birdie is telling you something in your inner ear about what you should let him do and what you should not let him do. That usually means you shouldn't let him do it. Don't talk yourself into compromising the love life that you have been dreaming about. Most women have the most respect for themselves the moment a guy says, "Hello! How are you?" After that, everything goes out the window. It's a hard world out there, ladies, and men are getting worse and worse and worse. The more women that allow themselves to believe that chivalry is dead, the worse guys are getting. The more women that allow themselves to believe that they have to prove themselves to a guy by showing him what "a good thing" he is missing by not spending time with you, then the more the guy is going to believe that he is all that, and every other woman is going to think the same as you are. It's very typical for a woman to think that if she loses weight, then she will get her confidence back. No! If you want to lose weight, fine, but always have confidence in yourself because, every time he is looking away from you, someone else will look your way. Always keep confidence in yourself, no matter how you look.

I hate to say this, but it seems to me that the best way to get a guy to really respect you in the beginning of a relationship is to be mean to him. I'm not talking about cursing him out and calling him out of his name. You don't have to fuss all the time and scream and yell to be mean either. But by saying "no" to most of his offers. If the offer involves him not working at keeping you interested, the answer is no. If the offer is, "come to my house," and you've only known him for one or two weeks, the answer is no. If the offer is to meet his parents, and it's only been a month or two, the answer is no. If the offer is let me take you on a vacation to the Bahamas or a cruise or any other travel plans, the answer is no. Most guys are going to try to sucker you into going somewhere that the both of you can be alone for an extended period of time, which allows him time to get you to feeling all romantic and intimate so that he can take advantage of you. Even if you say to yourself, "I could use the getaway," don't do it. You must give him the impression of respect. If this man has dated before, he is going to use every trick in the book, and make up some along the way, in order to get you to do something that he can be in control of. The answer, my dear, is still no. A movie? Yes. Dinner? Yes. A Play? Yes. A walk in the park? Yes. At night? No. Do things with him when other people are around. Don't give up any control of your surroundings. No control of your rest of the day. I know you hate to drive, but meet him there. Insist on split checks. It takes time to gain respect, and a free ride is not the ride you want to be on in order to gain that respect. And if he can't take that you are like that…then he isn't the one. This is how you filter out those control freaks.

Of course, he is going to say, "I'm starting to feel like you don't trust me," or something equivalent. Your answer is "I don't trust you. Trust is earned, and it takes more than a couple of weeks to earn it." I don't care if he is a nice guy, and you know his mom, and his sister introduced the two of you. Still no. Remember, if you are firm in the beginning of a relationship, he is going to remember that firmness later in the relationship. Your firmness is showing him you can be trusted. Your firmness is showing him you are a step above the rest of the women who easily fell for his game. And if you start thinking that you are just SO privileged to have someone like him even interested in you, then you're already going to lose this battle. You must have respect in yourself in order to keep any kind of respect that any man can possibly have for you.

You've heard the expression: "Be a strong black woman." Well, when working with men, race is irrelevant. You have to be a strong woman — period. No matter what color you are. You have to show your strength. It's not a battle of who is going to be the boss in the relationship. It's a stance that you take where you will not just accept anything that a man has to dish out because you feel you are so helpless without him. Men will push you to try and find out exactly how far they can go. Sometimes these reactions are done purposely, but oftentimes this reaction is a subconscious reaction. He can't help but to want to know how far he can go. We want to know just how far we can go in a relationship. We want to know what kind of woman we are dealing with. All men want a freak in bed, but we also want a lady. A good lady. A nice lady. And we want a woman who knows when and how to be a lady and when and how to be a freak. We want to be the sole beholder of this lady, especially that freaky part. We want to know if the lady is smart. We want to know if the woman can think for herself. Men have a tendency of wanting to test to see just how far he can take something, especially in the beginning of a relationship or sometimes midway through. There is no stopping this reaction, ladies. Expect it! If it sounds like a game and you don't have time for games, it's not a game. It's the way he is. Just be firm, speak your mind, and don't let him have too much of his way. These are only tests of respect. Tests of how he will respect you two years down the road. Trust me, when I say, he will remember how you scored. He will remember what he can do and what he cannot do. These are good things. These are things a man wants to know before he marries you. This is what he wants to know before he commits to you. Again I say that, if he has to go through all of this and he ends up marrying you, then logic tells him that another man wouldn't have stood a chance if he tried to take you away from him overnight.

That is being IN respect with you. That is the goal that you want for any man you date. The quicker you start saying yes to him will define the rest of that relationship. It will define exactly how much respect he has to show you. It will define how much respect he has to give you.

So ask yourself this? Is his respect for you worth a couple of free shots? Is it worth a one-night stand? Is it worth him seeing you as the lady that came out of her house to his house at three o'clock in the morning? After all, you are both grown adults here. Is his respect for you worth just a booty call? After all, you know someone who did it, and they ended up getting married, so now it's your time, right? Is his respect for you worth that justification? Come on. You're a smarter woman than that. You're attractive, and you better believe it. You don't want to end up a cougar, and if you already are, you don't want to end up … lonely. Smart, sexy, and then lonely.

Smart, Sexy, and Lonely

DINNER AND A MOVIE, BATH by candlelight, foot massage with vanilla bean lotion, wine with strawberries (occasionally, dipped in chocolate), hot oil baths, walks in the park, holding hands on the beach, making love till sunset, roses for no reason, dancing with no music, silent conversations, sweet seductions on the phone, camping in the backyard, balloons waiting in the car, picnic by candlelight, midnight breakfast just for two, wrestle-playing in the nude, blind folds and whipped cream, horseback riding, batting cages and go carts, a drive to the country, midnight basketball (one-on-one), an occasional compliment, a card expressing love and a host of other things that may impress the lady that many men are reluctant to talk to because of the upscale status she may have.

A host of women find themselves alone at home on many nights, desiring a man to comfort them or share the life they have built for themselves. Many of these women are beautiful and turn many heads everywhere they go. Oftentimes, they have given their number out on several occasions to men who quickly shy away from them after learning about her upscale status. She is educated. She is professional. She speaks proper English. She drives a nice car. She lives in a beautiful home. She wears expensive clothes. She is perhaps even Christian and prays for that special man to come into her life. She is ... lonely. She has dated several men, and of these men, the wealthy ones are too arrogant, the less wealthy are too insecure, the educated are too egotistical, and the less educated find her intimidating.

Many of these women have asked, "Why do some men find it intimidating to date a woman who is more educated or more successful than they are?" Well, if you look from the perspective of many men that fall into the "intimidated with a smarter or wealthier woman" category, they are accustomed to having to show off in order to impress a woman. From flashy jewelry to chromed-out cars. Mostly done to attract attention. This type of man's entire game is summed up by showing off the few things he has acquired thus far in his life. Compared to the type of men he has as his friends, he may have acquired a bit to be proud of. He has made what he has accomplished his treasure, and it prides him to see that impressed expression on a woman's face. Most of the women that he has been able to attract have less than what he has acquired, or maybe on some occasions, she may have nearly the same. His conversations, to her, are always mainly about himself and what he has or what he has done.

For this man, taking a woman to a fairly expensive dinner for two may be one of the highlights of his dating experience. Either that, or dinners of that kind are reserved for special days, like birthdays or Valentine's Day. To date a woman who has accomplished more than him, he believes that she has those types of dinners all the time, and his ego is not going to allow him to have her showing him the finer sides of life. To him, that's his job. This man feels that what he may consider as a highlight may be just a regular day to her. He feels that the requirements of keeping her happy are out of his current reach. Socially this man feels that he may not be able to keep up with a more educated woman during conversations. This man likes to be the information network of the relationship. He wants to be the teacher and the trainer. So the last thing he wants to hear is a woman telling him how to do everything that he already believes he knows how to do. He doesn't want to get into a relationship that is going to turn out as a lasting power struggle.

What most of these men who think on that level don't realize is that many women who fall into the "smart" and "lonely" category often don't require a man to supply them with as much as this man thinks he may have to supply. She wants a man to take charge in the relationship. She wants a man to be the leader and the teacher, and she is willing to stand by and respect his decisions whether she totally agrees with them or not. She will state her opinions only as an option and then let him be the man he needs to be by letting him make that final decision.

She doesn't necessarily need to be wined and dined every weekend. She doesn't have to have the big expensive dinners on a weekly basis. Most of these women will assist in protecting that "ego" that he denies having, yet is accustomed to. Oftentimes there is no limit to what she will do to help him protect it. She wants a man she can be proud of and if he just can't afford some of her requirements in his current status, she doesn't mind assisting. The important things that these women require are usually not available through the means of either money or education. The values of the things she will admire are far more valuable than what he may hold them to be.

Dinner and a movie, bath by candle light, body or foot massage with vanilla bean lotion, wine with strawberries (occasionally, dipped in chocolate), hot oil baths, walks in the park, holding hands at the beach, making love till sunset, roses for no reason, dancing with no music, silent conversations, sweet seductions on the phone, camping in the backyard, balloons waiting in the car, picnic by candlelight, midnight breakfast just for two, wrestle-playing in the nude, blindfolds and whipped cream, horseback riding, batting cages and go carts, a drive to the country, midnight basketball (one-on-one), an occasional compliment, a card expressing love, and a smile.

Digging for Gold

Just left home. Cell phone rings. Look at the caller ID. Private or unknown number. "Hello?" Click. They hung up. He ignores it. Minutes later, the phone rings again. "Hello?" Click. They hung up again. Finally, he arrives at work. Phone rings. "Hello?" Click! They hung up again. "Who the hell keeps calling and hanging up?" He says, "I don't have time for these games." He places the phone in his desk or on silent because he doesn't want to be disturbed like that when he's at work, especially not by some idiot who may just have the wrong number or even some stupid bill collector.

Hours later, he checks his phone. Five to ten missed calls. No messages. "What's up with that?" Caller ID still says unknown or private number. This isn't the first time that this has happen. In fact, it just may happen once a month or in some cases weekly. He thinks about changing his phone number, or he may have even changed it. But regardless, it still happens.

Let's fast-forward to the weekend. The two of you spend some quality time together. Visit to the mall, park, club, or some other public spot. The two of you enjoy making the other laugh or smile by making observant comments about the different types of people you may pass by. He comments about the really overweight woman that passes by or the anorexic lady that's drinking a diet cola. The both of you giggle about the orange polka-dot dress on the flat, ironing board butt, middle-aged woman with the purple hat. But the big booty, perfectly curved with the form fitted pants and the low-cut, see-through white nylon shirt, with no bra underneath wearing girl didn't earn him a laugh, a smile, a grin or even a chuckle when he commented on how underdressed and tacky she was in this public place. It only got him a cold stare or jab in his side. Yes, that unknown lady may even have led you two into an hour-long conversation on how disrespectful he is or how you felt he really wished you wouldn't have been with him at the time because he may have said something to the stranger, as if, he always flirts with other women while you aren't around.

These are all signs of a relationship that has no business going on any longer. In fact, the time you are spending together is only time you could be spending with the real person that you are going to end up with sooner or later. These small instances are the tell-tell signs of what is going to be either a long relationship of future cheating or a marriage of many and constant fights. Though only a few examples have been supplied here, many signs are available to help you in determining the outcome of a relationship where one person is constantly being accused of cheating when he or she is, in fact, not cheating.

These situations can be identified by many men who have suffered this in a relationship. Perhaps some women have been put into this situation, as well, or you are the woman who has done this to your mate. If you didn't pick up on the unknown phone call illustrations provided in the first paragraph, then you are surely clueless on the many "behind your back" investigative antics you or your mate is performing to dig up trash on you. Whether you are doing something or not behind your mate's back, this is a prime clue that you are in for a MAJOR HORROR in some point in your relationship.

If someone is checking to break your voice mail pass code to your cell phone, or how many minutes you use in a month and checking the different numbers that you call, then you need to take heed. If they are going through your bills and trying to sneak through your purse or wallet or, to top it off, checking to see how many miles you've added from one day to another on your car's odometer, then you need to just leave that relationship IMMEDIATELY. I'm not talking about a relationship where one of you has already cheated on the other and you are now trying to make it work by building and proving trust. No. I'm talking about when it's a fairly new relationship, and these accusations are just developing out of the blue or even due to someone getting hurt in a previous relationship and now they're dragging that history into this new one.

If anyone takes the time to overanalyze everything you do, every way you say hello to someone, or every time you so happen to look in a general direction and get accused of doing something behind his or her back, then once again I suggest that you leave that person alone. Chances are that, in their minds, they will find evidence that you are guilty. Note the phrase "in their minds." For example, if someone introduces you to someone, whom they have told you over and over again that this person is a liar, you are going to expect, when you finally meet that person, that they are lying about everything they tell you about themselves. You only see what you have been expecting to see. So in this same way, your mate will only see what they are looking to find. They do find exactly what they are looking for because they will turn every situation they see into evidence to use against you.

You are most likely wasting your time with that person. The odds will be against you if you plan on changing that person's way of thinking. This person's mind has been burned into being too suspicious. In that relationship, you will only be a therapist. Not a lover. It will take too much time and commitment to help teach that person what trust is all about. They are going to have to learn that lesson from losing you or someone else. And staying just because the sex is good is only setting you up for more and more drama with this person.

You can try and talk it over or even share this with that person to give them a hint of the hell you are going through with them or even express the decision that you must make about the relationship to them. It still will most likely not work. But, if you decide to stay in that relationship, then it's not because of some comfortable future with that person that has made you stay. It's simply a "hold the phone until someone else calls" situation, because you are afraid to be alone, afraid to have no one to call on when that horniness or loneliness kicks in.

Be alone. It's fair to you and that person to end things early rather than drag it on for more months or more weeks or even more days with more accusations and more excuses. Many times, at the very early stages of a relationship, guys sometime tend to think this jealous behavior is cute, but after a while, that cuteness is going to turn into a living nightmare.

For the ladies that continue to investigate or interrogate a non-cheating man, it will eventually lead to an all-out assault on an attempt for him to just go for it. You were digging to find gold, and he is going to eventually place that gold there for you to find. If you are going to be accusing him anyways, he is going to think to himself that he may as well just do it. And if he does do it, guess who he is going to blame? You! His excuse is going to be, you made him do it because you kept accusing him of doing it. He's going to say that he hadn't done anything beforehand but since he was living the life of a cheater anyways without receiving any of the benefits of a cheater than he may as well fill that void that you made up in your mind. He's going to get drunk enough to do it and use that drunken state as another part of the fuel to set fire to an excuse to finally do it, and odds are it will be with somebody that you both know.

That will be a reasonable excuse for him. He may even have warned you he was going to do it one day if you didn't stop accusing him. You tried to stop, but you couldn't, so the digging started again. All this because you truly were not ready to go into a relationship in the first place due to perhaps that past history in your previous relationship or because you have this string of jealousy inside you that you just cannot shed. To place that burden on another is not fair, especially if that other person is genuinely innocent. So before accusing your mate of being a cheater with absolutely no proof, you need to understand how to recognize the real signs that he is cheating.

Signs That Your Man is Cheating

DESPITE THE MANY PUBLISHED LISTS titled "How to Tell if Your Man is Cheating," I boldly disagree with most of them. Furthermore, I categorize these lists as not "signs that your man is cheating" but rather "how to make a woman paranoid." Now before you get your pencil and pen ready and put on your detective gear, remember much of these so-called signs can be avoided if you first study the "Faithful as you Want" section of this book. Many good men turn into cheaters because of the "lack of" treatment that you give. Call it an excuse if you want, but that is his reasoning. I'm not talking about every single man that cheats. Some men are born cheaters and refuse to have just one single woman, even after marriage. Here, I'm addressing men who really don't want to cheat and don't have that history of cheating but find themselves cheating anyway.

Now let's get directly to the point. First I need you to consider the times when your man would bitch and complain about what you are not doing to keep him, as warnings instead of complaints. You know those repetitive comments he makes about having to do so many things for himself as if he was single. The late nights he finds himself up alone wishing you were there giving him "special" attention. Those many times when you were sick or tired and didn't feel like it and he just rolled over angry until he fell asleep. Those times when no kiss was waiting for him when he got home from a long, hard day. Instead of kisses, all he hears are complaints about how you have been so busy all day and all he has to do is go to work and come home. Even if you both work, he still has given hints or complained about something he wants or expects when he comes home. After a number of years of those signs and complaints, he may cave in to getting attention elsewhere. He doesn't have to look far to become a cheater. After going through so much non-attentiveness from you, any attention from anybody else is going to attract him.

I'm sure there are many ladies who are reading this who know exactly what I'm talking about. Everybody complains about something in a relationship. I'm sure you have your complaints, too. Focus on those legitimate complaints that you know deep down in your heart that your man is right about. You know when you are not right. You know when you have not been doing what you used to do in the earlier stages of the relationship. I know you may have your reasons for why you stopped, and you may blame him or other things to justify your actions, but when your man starts getting interested in someone else, I assure you, you are going to wish that you never stopped or had not waited so long to put that stubborn attitude behind you.

But it's not just the non-attentiveness that will make a man start cheating on his lady. It's the lack of taking care of yourself like you used to. You don't dress the same. You don't act the same, and now you don't look the same. You talk down about the latest fashions that he sees other women wearing. You have introduced him to a new woman, and he doesn't like it. But he tries to like it. Sometimes he doesn't even realize what is missing in the relationship, but he knows that something is missing. Remember, ladies, this man goes out of the house everyday and is surrounded by other women who are dressing and looking their best. But when he comes home to you from all that buffet outside, you're only dressed like a sandwich. Your man wants to come home to a woman like the ones he has been passing by all day. But I hear you out there, ladies.

I hear you saying he has no business even looking at those other women. My dear, instead of complaining about what he is looking at and what he is not looking at, you should be looking as well and taking note of what your man does and does not like. Yes, it can be disrespectful at times, but don't forget that view that he was checking out. Duplicate it. He was looking at her for a reason, and it's not always that "he wants to sleep with her" reason you invented. He looks because it's attractive to him. In his mind, it's not taking anything away from you or his opinion of you. No matter how sweet you may think it is that your man doesn't look at other women while he is with you, men are very visually, and if something is attractive, it's just attractive. Some women relate the word attractive to "wanting to have sex with." It doesn't. It means appealing to the eyes. It doesn't mean he wants her over you. In fact, ladies, believe it or not, if you are more cool about your man glancing at a passing by women that is attractive, and if you both comment on it, the more comfortable it is going to make your man and the more unbelievably awesome he is going to think you are. I'm not trying to sell you on letting your man look at other women all the time; I'm just stating a perspective on how men think and how, based on your reactions, you can gain the benefit of getting more communication out of your man by allowing yourself to become his best friend as both a lover and a mate, as well as like one of his guy friends.

A woman who is cool and shows confidence in herself by not tripping over some good-looking women in a far off distance is more apt to attract the interest and commitment of a man. A woman who turns on a radar for every other pretty woman in the area and who watches and keeps an eye on her man to see if he is going to look is only going to get angry or feel disrespected because she feels he just can't stop staring.

I know you want your man to think you are the only woman on the planet. But get back to reality. YOU ARE NOT. And based on how you carry yourself, you remind him of that every single day when he hits the door. Now before you go into thinking how much you do for your man and how he should be appreciative, he is. But he can't help being visually attracted to other women. He will fight it. Very hard! But if you are slacking on reassuring yourself of how beautiful you are and showing him how beautiful that you are and actually believing you are, he is going to find himself in a position of pursuing someone else. Believe it or not, ladies, some men really, really, really don't want to cheat. Just because a man sees a very attractive woman, it doesn't mean that he wants to sleep with her, but if you are one of those women that always accuses him of wanting to, then one day he will. Again I say, when you always accuse a man of doing something and he is not doing anything, you are pretty much cheerleading him into doing it. After all, you are basically putting him in the bed with another woman, so he may as well do it. Thus, if you are always saying that he is. STOP. Most men translate your accusations into permissions. And the woman he is going to end up cheating on you with will be the woman who has confidence in herself of knowing she's beautiful, and feel she is qualified to keep your man's interest at all times. You will only be seen as the one who does not realize what she has because you are not able to completely satisfy him.

    Now for the man that has already been pushed over that edge to cheat, there are some signs that you will be able to see. I'm not going to mention the obvious signs of lipstick on his collar or perfume on his skin. Those are standard signs that you should be aware of, and even though you are aware of them, I already know that most of the women that are reading this have heard of a good excuse as to why the lipstick was there and why the perfume smell is there. After all, there ARE times that a woman may give him a hug or he brush into someone in a crowded room, right? Right? Yeah … right.

    Well, ladies, here is a true sign. If all of a sudden your man starts buying you flowers or gifts when he hasn't bought those flowers or gifts for a long time before, that's a sign. If he hasn't been buying them out of love in all this time, then guilt is usually the next reason. And usually, when you get that gift, it means that he has cheated either the night he gave you the gift, or the night before. If he didn't actually cheat, then he just left a date or had a really damn good time with someone else.

If your man starts finding creative ways to get you to start spending more time by yourself when at first he didn't want you to, that's a sign. The time you are spending by yourself is the time he is spending with someone else. Now don't get this confused with your man being interested in you meeting some female friends to hang out with, instead of you and him spending so much time together. Oftentimes, there are men who are concerned that their woman isn't socializing with any of her girlfriends anymore. Sometimes a man really wants to spend some time with his buddies and may actually feel bad that you are not out there spending some time with some of your girlfriends. But if your man has a history of always spending time with you and now he is trying to pull away, you may want to evaluate what he is up to.

When your man starts questioning you about where you've been, how long did it take you, and who you've been talking to on the phone, that's a sign. A paranoid man is usually paranoid because he thinks you're doing what he is doing. His conscience turns on his suspicions toward you doing what he is doing. However, if you are in the very beginning stages of a relationship and your man starts off this relationship treating you like this, then this man has either been cheated on before or has a history of being a cheater. Either way, this will become very annoying to you after you've really invested a lot of time in this relationship. You can't start off a relationship not trusting someone. You should take this as a sign to slow things down, or bail out before you invest your time into it.

For the long term relationships where your man was not asking you all these types of questions before and now all of a sudden he is laying this "where you been" attitude on you, then you may want to open your eyes and investigate what he is doing. That is in case you are really doing something that you don't want your man to know about.

If your man has never been the type to carry cash all the time and now all of a sudden you start finding wads of cash in his wallet, this is a sign. Generally, if you and him are both looking at your accounts and managing your finances, your man doesn't want to leave any type of trails behind where you can track where he is spending his money. If he is taking someone out a lot or spending any type of money on her, he will most likely use cash, instead of a credit card. This way, he can throw away the receipt, so there will be no trace of where he spent the money. ATM withdrawals can always be explained for something else, so don't think you can corner him on that one. Also, if you have only seen one time where your man has had an excess amount of cash in his wallet, that doesn't mean he is cheating. So don't start getting paranoid over a single incident. But keep your eyes open. He could also be experimenting in some of those happy ending massage parlors. Those should be considered cheating as well. Don't let him explain it otherwise.

If your man has a habit of always turning his cell phone off when he comes home (Do I seriously have to write about this?), then it's obvious that he is hiding something. The excuse of him not wanting to be bothered at home from his job is, hmm, lame. You'd have to be a complete idiot to fall for something like that, especially when it wasn't a problem before. Now, if you have been paranoid that your man has been cheating and if you have started checking his phone for numbers and trying to unlock his code and he has caught you doing that, then that could definitely be a reason for him to lock or turn off his phone from you. Not necessarily to hide something from you, but to keep himself from having to explain to you every single phone entry. Men don't like to feel as if they are being investigated. It's cute in the beginning to him, but when you keep accusing your man of doing something and he isn't, then (here I go again telling you as before) you are only cheering him on to actually do something behind your back. Men are not attracted to paranoid women.

Sometimes we will put up with it for a while, especially if he is guilty of something, but if he isn't guilty, he will most likely find a girlfriend who isn't paranoid and then eventually start having a relationship with her and leave you. There is a fine line from being suspicious that your man is cheating on you and being a paranoid woman. If it is strictly paranoia, then every thing you see or hear this guy do or say is going to register in your mind as a clue that he is cheating. If you are that kind of woman, then you need to be single for a little longer until you can build up more confidence in yourself to truly believe that you have a lot to offer someone else and the other person will not have to look around for someone else to replace you. Yes, replace, because men don't generally break up with a woman, unless he already has someone else in mind. It's hard for the average man to simply go cold turkey with no one in his life.

Do these two phrases sound familiar? "I had a big lunch" or "I picked up a bite after work." If you've heard these phrases or similar a few times within the same week, then that's a sign that he just came from someone else's house or just had dinner with someone else. Ask yourself if your man has a history of skipping dinner with you. Usually the first thing a man wants to do after he comes home from work is eat. Know his routine and be suspicious if it is starting to change. Don't let the excuse of watching his weight fly either. You may have read somewhere else that a sign for a man who is cheating is for him to start getting in shape or dieting. I don't agree. If he is on some kind of new health kick and is trying to lose weight, then that isn't necessarily a sign. In this day and age, everyone is trying to get in shape. You should notice if, when the two of you are together, he is attempting to change his eating habits and is sometimes struggling while doing it. If so, then it's fair to assume he is not lying about not wanting to eat too much sometimes at home. But you should see signs of him struggling to keep that healthy eating diet or see signs that he is succeeding in it. If he only says that when he comes home from work, then watch out. Don't you think it's weird that you can spend all day Saturday and Sunday with him and he has not complained about eating junk, but all of a sudden, after work, when he comes home, he doesn't want to eat anything at home? Think about it. And prepare for the "I don't diet on weekends" excuse.

Now that you have evidence

During any accusation that you make to him about cheating on you, always keep your composure and your self-esteem in tack. As much as it may hurt, try to keep your cool while you are about to accuse him of anything. Don't let thoughts of him cheating on you lower your self-esteem. Don't start thinking that there is something wrong with you that led him into cheating on you. If he detects that you feel that way, then he will use your weakness as an excuse for driving him to do that. The very moment that you start accusing him, he will instantly start reading you to find something to backup his point of view or an escape route to steer you off track. Men are masters at turning things around, so get your facts straight and your evidence together. If you lose your cool, you can prepare to also lose the argument.

If, for some reason, he does reveal that you are part of the blame, and oftentimes when a good man has cheated, then you very well could be part of the blame from his perspective, then it would be fair to listen to his perspective on that. There may be some truth heard here because, many of times, a good man can be forced to cheat. You may not agree with that, but if your man has been communicating with you about how unhappy he is, and in return, you have done nothing about it, then eventually he is going to start telling his problems to someone else, and she will listen. Also because she is listening and you are not, then he will start to develop feelings for her. You do not want that to happen because, believe it or not, regardless of what you may have heard, men can actually love two women at the same time. It may not be the same kind of love, but the emotion is still there. He will love one for something and the other for something else, and that is an addictive feeling for a man where the guilt that he feels for doing that will be pushed to the side because it will be hard for him to go back to settling for one person to fulfill his needs. Get it off your mind that those "needs" are strictly sexual because it is not. Sex is not the only reason that a man will cheat on you. It is whatever your relationship is lacking the most. It is whatever he has been trying to communicate with you about. It is those needs that you have been ignoring. That is the primary reason that he is cheating on you. In that case, sex will just be a side effect of that action. That is if sex is even involved in that other relationship, and it's rare that it's not. Regardless if it is or not, if he is lying to spend time with someone else, it's cheating. Remember that.

You need to make a decision for yourself as to if you want to keep your man or let him go. It's going to be a hard decision for you to make, especially if you caused some of this by ignoring some of his desires. It is very possible that you will win that battle and get your man back, but in order to do that, you are going to have to make some changes in that relationship and, again, keep your composure. Don't start yelling so much and fighting, although that may be your first reaction, so try to calm down and have a level head about it. Try to make a logical decision about your next actions versus an emotional decision. Yes, I know, that's extremely hard to do.

Whatever you decide, don't try to compete with the other woman. Just try to be a better you. Being a better you can be something that you can keep up for a long time, but trying to compete with the other woman and changing your ways to be more like her is just fooling yourself. You will not be able to keep that up for very long. Plus your man wants a real woman, not some actress who is only filling a role. You have to want to do things for your man and not be forced to do it, or it will mean nothing. I'm sure you can identify with that because, in the same way, it means a lot more to you if a man gives you flowers at will versus you asking him to buy you some flowers.

If you feel that you have been nothing but a good woman to him and still he has crossed over to cheating with someone else, then you need to really look at that relationship and it's future. Some women I have spoken to go by the "slip up one time rule." That's where you allow a one-time slip up for a guy, give him another chance, but if he does it again, then kick him to the curve. You are going to have to decide if that method will work for you. Although some relationships can survive after an infidelity has taken place, some women are constantly letting themselves get hurt, over and over again. They start accepting that a man will always cheat and feel pride in the fact that he keeps coming back home to her. Please, ladies, don't fall into that trap. There ARE good men out there, some who have been trained by being cheated on and some that just need a little touch up training from you.

Regardless of the situation, always fall in love with you first. If you love yourself and show it, you will gain his respect. Remember respect is different from love for a man. Allowing him to come back into your life after cheating on you does show how much you love him, but in the ultimate view of things, it's the greatest loss of respect. Deep inside, he is going to feel he got away with it. He's going to have the palm of the hand type of satisfaction. In some cases, a man will see his life flash before his eyes and realize how bad he messed up and is totally lucky that you accepted him back. But that got away with it feeling … will still be there even if he buries it and never admits it. Those feelings he had for the other girl … yes … they will still exist. They will eventually pass, though, especially if there are kids involved where he is a good father to them and an overall good man at heart. But if it's just the two of you, with no kids involved … the chances of him not cheating again is like the odds of winning a major lotto.

Denial! A very powerful word. Many women are so guilty of this when they have undisputable evidence that their man is cheating. Not only is she in denial, but she will come up with ways to defend the actions of her man where he doesn't even have to answer to any of the accusations. In fact, I know a woman who went and parked in front of her boyfriend's house when she couldn't reach him after calling all day. She saw shadows in the window of two people and a strange car in the driveway. She continued to call him, even while she was parked in front of his house, but he would not answer the phone. She had a girlfriend of hers in the car with her who begged her to knock on the door, yet she refused. She told her friend that he must not be home, but at work and had someone house sitting for him. House sitting? This was her story! When he finally called her THE NEXT MORNING, he started the conversation off with "I'm sorry I missed your call last night, but I was sleeping." Sleeping? Yeah, with someone else.

Ladies, don't make excuses for your man. Don't even hint to a reason as to what he has been up to. Don't start off like, "Wow! You must have been really tired. I called you all night long." Of course, he is going to say, "Yeah, I was, I really knocked out and didn't hear a thing." Don't play games, ladies, if you think he is cheating. Don't try to plot to see if you can catch him. Just straight up tell him, "I think you are cheating." Tell him you don't want to hear any excuses. Instead just have him state his case. Have him tell you what's really been going on. Tell him to be honest and to level with you. You need to be serious when expressing that. If he starts with the "how can you question me like that" crap or the "I deserve to know why you are asking me this" crap, then just say, "Forget it. I need some time to myself, and I'll let you know when I feel like talking to you." If you are not married and live separately, then don't talk to him for a week. He's going to try to stop you from leaving or turning away, but repeat yourself, and be firm about not talking about it. Make him sweat, and if he is guilty, after some time, he will start coming to you with "was it that time when…" or "are you talking about when…."

After a week of him leaving messages and wondering why you are acting distant or tripping, you are then ready to hold that conversation. But you need to stay strong before that point and don't give in to his pleas.

If you are married or live in the same house, this is going to be a bit harder, but you need to shut down. You need to speak in short sentences to the point of ignoring him. Only say, "I will talk to you about you when I am ready." After a week of this, then you are ready to talk about it. When you do start to talk about it, don't let him twist it to "he" isn't ready to talk about it. Don't let him try what you just did. It's important that you stay in control of that conversation logically and not emotionally. Stay logical because he is going to have conjured up a really good excuse for whatever proof you have to show or say. But remember, you still haven't told him about any evidence you may have. You still haven't given up any clues as to what you are talking about, and it's been eating at him to the point that he may even be pissed off about it. He may be ready to rage about it to get to you. Don't be surprised if he tries twisting this time to a time where he was in control of the conversation. Remember, for most men, they are going to dominate the conversation. Don't let him. This is your moment. This is your time to get answers. Take any refusal to have that conversation with you as a sign of him being guilty of something.

After all is said and done, and he has either confessed or has proven himself to be innocent, then you will, at least, have gained a new understanding in your relationship and a new level of respect. He will respect you more for the way you handled that whether he was guilty or innocent. And remember, respect is always what you want from him first, and then love.

Designed for Cheating On

Judging by the reactions of people who have just received the news that their significant other has been cheating on them with someone else, you would think that adultery or "messing around" was a new form of cancer that they have just been notified about receiving. The news is received as either a shock or as the final end to a heavily investigated theory that, in either case, leaves them in a state of rage and anger that will drive them to a fury of emotional destruction. This is an understandable reaction, and many would not question the reaction or vengeance that those individuals would want to take against that person that they have shared and sacrificed so much of their lives for and time with. In exchange for all of the love and the giving of themselves sexually and emotionally, financially and spiritually, physically and mentally, their significant other would have the nerve to sleep with somebody else.

No one should have to go through that kind of torture! No one deserves to have his or her heart trampled on like that! And why would you even consider forgiving somebody like that! It's not your fault that they can't control themselves! You are the victim here! Cheating is totally unacceptable! And I, as the author of this, totally agree with you!

BUT!

There are some women, and some men *WHO ARE DESIGNED TO BE CHEATED ON.*

What must a mate do to get their partner to truly understand the life that they are putting the other through when they have to ask them to do the obvious? It's often said that communication is the key to any happy and lasting relationship, but why must someone have to continually communicate a desire or expectation over and over again. At some point to ask to be treated how you would like to be treated makes it irrelevant for your mate to do anything for you simply because you always have to ask for it. To put it simply, if you have to ask your mate to get you something on special days like Valentine's Day, birthdays, or anniversaries, then it really doesn't mean as much when they do it. It would mean a whole lot more if you didn't have to ask for it in the first place. Now don't get me wrong, I definitely promote the act of letting someone know your likes and dislikes so that they can do their part in satisfying your needs, but no one should have to constantly remind their mate what it takes to show a little affection and appreciation. How you like to be treated is something that is talked about in the beginning of a relationship, not something that needs to be reinforced three years later over and over again.

Can you personally identify with any of these examples?

If you pick up some food on the way home, and you know your mate hasn't eaten and is also on the way home from work or somewhere else, is it necessary for him or her to have to ask you to bring something for them? Do you even know what their favorite food item is from the short menus from those repetitive fast food chains?

Have you learned any of his or her habits other than the mess you want to hold onto and use as ammo on your next bitch session?

If your mate wanted to make love to you the night before and you claim you were too tired or sick (or whatever made up excuse you gave him or her), does your mate have to ask for it again the next night, or are you going to volunteer? Will you be the initiator of that sexual act?

If you know your partner is feeling sick, does he or she have to ask you to take care of him or her, especially with most men because you know how much of a baby they can be when they are sick?

When your mate complains about an ache or pain, do you take over the conversation to talk about your own ache or pain that you been having, thus completely stealing his or her moment?

Have you noticed that he or she has been wearing the same outfits every time you go out on the town together and it's been a year already and you have the nerve to spend every extra dime on yourself and not even buy a tie for him or a pair of stockings for her?

Do you only wash clothes when YOU need some underwear? Have you ever washed only one item in the washer when a stack of clothes needs to be washed?

Do you only buy groceries when YOUR snacks run out?

Do you only wash your car and leave the one right next to it dirty?

Does your mate have to always ask for foreplay or is it volunteered?

If you're a stay-at-home spouse, do you ever walk him or her to the door when he or she is leaving for work?

Have you ever surprised him or her with a candlelight dinner?

Have you ever showed up with only a coat and no clothes underneath?

Have you ever pleased him or her sexually without wanting something in return, just to make sure you are keeping him or her well pleased regularly? Have you ever gone down on your mate without expecting the favor to be returned?

Do you even get where I'm going with all of this yet? Must I say it in layman's terms? *DO YOU HAVE ANY COMPASSION FOR YOUR MATE WHATSOEVER?* Do you ever go completely out of your way to make your mate totally happy without getting something out of it in return?

Compassion! A lack of it in a relationship is a major key to designing your own cheating spouse. There is a lot of heavy frustration going on in the heart of the receiver of the NOTHINGS that you are supplying in that relationship. So what if you get along well! So what about the times you two laugh and talk together! So what if the sex is great (when you finally have it)! So what if you have modern material items and fancy crap throughout the home! So what if your family likes your mate because of his or her crazy sense of humor! So what if they take care of you well and you never really have to worry about bills! So what if you've been together for more than three years! So what if you are faithful! So what if you are better off than a lot of people you know! Odds are that, at this point, you had less to do with it than your mate! It is your mate that has been keeping all of it going. And if not, you only bought something to the table only after your mate bitched about it afterwards. Is this person I'm talking about you?

So as a result of all the pressure that comes with dealing with the balancing of YOUR good life and HIS OR HER sacrificing, your mate is both consciously, as well as subconsciously, feeling a need of another to supply what is missing out of his or her life, and oftentimes, it's because of a lack of compassion. That feeling of being appreciated if that person feels that he or she has been giving so much for the other person's comfort. He or she became the sacrificial lamb for you. The one that has been the most compassionate one and has been carrying the heart of the relationship.

When someone who is full of compassion gets involved with someone who lacks the simplest of compassion, it's a sure setup for that compassionate person to be forced to receive appreciation from someplace else. All a compassionate person wants in return for his or her sacrifices is to feel appreciated. And if you are not being thoughtful enough to show that appreciation by sacrificing, at least, an additional 10 percent of your time, body, and mind exclusively for that person on a weekly bases, then 100 percent of that person is going to be shared with somebody else. Not because they want to, but because you may be, in essence, forcing them to regardless of whether you are ready to admit that or not.

This is not an excuse for the cheaters out there, but an awakening for those who are out there and are not putting forth the efforts to keep a balance in that relationship. You have to show compassion in your daily life with a person who has been showing compassion to you. If you are with a giver, then you need to be a good receiver, and you need to learn how to appreciate what your mate has to give. A giver in a relationship doesn't always say how he or she wants to be treated; instead this person will show it by doing unto you. When you fail to reciprocate that, in due time, he or she will receive appreciation from another. An appreciation that starts with just a "thank you" or "how is your day" from someone else. An appreciating that includes taking some time to just listen to the other talk about his or her problems or anything that is on his or her mind.

If you are in a relationship and you are the one that lacks compassion, then your mate is going to be left longing for it in any form that he or she can receive it in. After not having it, yet giving it, it's very possible that someone else out there is going to show it and it doesn't even have to be purposely done. You raised the net, and now fish are jumping in. "Thank you" and "aww, you're so nice" is going to be received as heartfelt. The next thing your mate's going to know is he or she is going to start liking it from that someone else and it's going to end up becoming outright fun flirting.

Your mate just found a friend that is showing appreciation from the compassion your mate genuinely has, but you have failed to show appreciation. It doesn't start with anything sensual but just small things. Things such as your mate going out for lunch and asking anyone if they want him or her to bring something back, and that one co-worker that was in a meeting at the time didn't hear it yet your mate decided to be nice and bring him or her a sandwich back. The co-worker was overjoyed and bombarded your mate with "thank yous" and "you didn't have tos" and "oh my that was so sweets," so the next morning, your mate receives something special in return or even a little rose on the desk with a thank you card. Little things like that are how it all starts. So it continues. And continues, till it's, again, outright fun flirting.

All of this could be avoided if they are used to getting appreciation from you. It wouldn't mean as much to him or her if you showered your mate with appreciation all the time. It would be a routine for him or her and your significant other would love it. Your mate will love you even more for never stopping at doing those little things, the little things of compassion and appreciation that cause you to not be one of those that are designed to be cheated on.

Es-E-Ex

"Men are to sex like women are to shoe shopping." (This quote excludes pros and hoes.)

With this understanding, men have been able to get out of many sticky situations with their woman whenever she has found out or has come close to finding out that her man has been seeing another female. For the most part, it is not the female that has a clear understanding of this, but it is the male that understands it and has to try to explain that difference in order to straighten things out. No matter how hard the explanation is for him to explain, somehow the female usually will accept it or deal with it, resulting in her giving him another chance. Contrary to what many women would say after reading this, they WILL usually bend, at least once, for a cheating man, especially if the man can explain his situation with confidence and efficiency.

Men perceive sex at a much different level than how women perceive sex. Not that one is greater than the other; they are just different. When the average man has sex, there's not usually any type of confirmation that goes along with it. For most men, the sexual experience is like relieving an itch. No feelings have to be associated with it. It was itching, and scratching made it feel better. He was horny, and sex solved it. Now women get horny, and sex solves it, too, but like I said with a man it's like an itch, so it really doesn't matter as to how it stops itching, as long as the itch goes away. For the record, that cold shower crap doesn't work because men are SO visual that, as soon as he see any form that even resembles a woman, he becomes itchy again. So when it really gets bad, it doesn't even matter if she is attractive or not. As long as she is clean, that will usually certify it as a "go, go, go, go, go!"

Women, on the other hand, have a whole lot more restraint. Just like it has been said that women can endure more pain than a man, such as childbirth, a woman can also endure longer durations of no sex than the average man can. Part of this logic is how women perceive the sexual experience. Sex equals love, caring, commitment, trust, attraction, reliability, and oftentimes, they all go hand-in-hand together for the "average" woman. You may pick one of those words from that list at any time to exclude, and the others will still be necessary to define how the average women will have the act of sex with someone, thus the remaining words will make up for the word that is taken out. (Confusing, huh?) All of those complexities are not necessary for a man to sleep with someone. A woman can mess around and will eventually start developing emotions for the one she is messing around with. For a man, sex and emotions are completely separate entities.

The trade-off for a man to have emotions for a woman isn't necessarily the sexual experience. When emotions develop for the male, he starts rearranging how he spends his money and time. This is different from simply giving a woman money or buying her nice things, which is what a man may do when he is just trying to get some. The portion of money management he is willing to do when he starts falling in love with a woman includes instances where he is taking care of her personal responsibilities. Thus, paying her bills, rent, mortgage, car note, etc. If the man doesn't have any money to spend, then the trade off is usually a troth of household chores. This will include tasks like cleaning the house, cooking, washing clothes, doing the dishes, cutting the lawn, and even babysitting kids that are not even his. It can get pretty pathetic for a man when he falls in love with a woman. This is why, when a man IS caught in the act of messing around, he somehow always quotes the cheating cliché: "It didn't mean anything."

So it's the male's job to explain what the hell is meant by "it didn't mean anything." It's a pretty hard job to explain even with the knowledge of knowing that a woman's perception of sex is different than a man's. Educating her isn't an easy task in the middle of a heated argument. A man is really going to have to be on the top of his conversation in order to get himself out of this one, especially with a woman that hasn't accepted or understood the differences between how the two regard sex whether she agrees or disagrees with it.

Now for the woman that already understands this, there really is no explanation required on the part of the male. All she wants is two things:

1.) To know what she wasn't doing enough of to satisfy him. This isn't because she wants to improve anything, but because she feels that she has already done enough for his sorry ass (as she may put it) for him to do this to her.

2.) Begging and pleading. She wants him to assume the dog's position and put her in the position of master. This is similar to the position that she met him in when she held the reigns to the relationship. She had something that he wanted, and he displayed that to her all the time during that "impress her stage." Now he's gotten so comfortable with her that he has taken the crown off her head and placed himself on a throne, where she isn't his queen but his subject. He must now give her BACK the crown AND the throne and BEG like a dog to win her back.

Now the hard part for the male is to avoid all of this and not cheat at all. To most women that sound like an easy solution; however, from the perspective of many men, that's a massive task to avoid, especially men in the position of power and fame. That power or fame can be found in many lifestyles, not just your millionaires or celebrities. It can be found in doctors, lawyers, managers, preachers, teachers, coaches, small or large business owners, and even supervisors. Basically any position one can obtain where people can look up to you. Many women find it attractive to be with someone that has a respectable position or career. The men in uniform. The men in law enforcement or firefighting. So often they find themselves with offers of sex and flirtatiousness thrown right in their faces. Opportunities don't exist as much for those who aren't in those types of careers. Understand that the average attractive female is accustomed to getting some kind of the same attention or more as a powerful male. They have received that attention from all of their earlier developing teenage years and throughout their adult lives. But open advances are rarer for men than it is for women. (Even though that male that has been working out to achieve the body of a male god may disagree.)

Regardless of all of that, cheating is not impossible. It takes a lot of work and commitment on the sides of both parties in that relationship. Using sex as a weapon can and will eventually backfire on that relationship. Saying "no" when the other is clearly in heat for sex can develop into a bad habit. That man is only going to settle for masturbation for only so long. Your motionless sex is eventually going to make him lose interest. Your dry hand job while you're reading a book or watching TV is eventually going to leave you watching TV and reading while someone else is actually paying attention to what you aren't doing.

That quickie for her is eventually going to come back and slap him in the face. If he hasn't learned by now, he better learn how to please her. He needs to listen to her body. Learn her moans, grunts, and groans. She may not always tell him what she wants and, sometimes, may not even know what will get her there. Odds are what he's learned came from porno and isn't what real women actually want. If he wants to learn how to lick her right, he may switch to being taught by some lesbian porn instead. He may try asking her to guide him on how she wants it done. Sexual satisfaction, sometimes, requires training for both parties by one another.

And if any guys are reading this, just because you are erect and ready to roll, doesn't mean you can just jump on top of her and pump into three minutes of ecstasy. Rest assured, you're only pushing her away into her own moments of ecstasy without you. Ha! In comparison to a male thinking that masturbation is pleasing to him, most women can do themselves ten times better than a man ever could the moment he leaves after his failed attempt at pleasing her. You should not let your woman's self-pleasuring end up being better at pleasing her than you.

In the same way, ladies, do not let your man's self-pleasuring take your place. He would much rather you touch him in every way possible than for him to do it himself. Keep your man worn out sexually, and you can assure a more faithful relationship.

True Identity

I'm hoping that not many people can identify with this. Even though I'm sure that there are more people going through this, my wishes are that there aren't very many. There are people who have somewhat involuntarily presented themselves to be someone in a relationship that they truly are not, and they did not purposely intend to camouflage themselves in the relationship on a permanent basis.

Most people who are "living a single life" situation want to meet that someone special and attempt to present themselves as "putting their best foot forward." This has been a common practice for decades where you increase your politeness level by 60 percent, along with your manners, ethical standards, social skills, outside appearances, dress code, patience and eating rituals. After that first impression routine has been used to impress that Olympic hopeful that we have, at some point, attracted, the day finally comes where you get the opportunity to flourish for him or her in an agreed setting, which is commonly known as a "date."

People en masse perform this ritual of meeting someone, and of course, everyone understands that the real person from that date will soon show his or her true face little by little as the days and weeks go by. You prepare yourself for that reality because the truth is that nobody is perfect and really truly can't conform themselves to be that "everything I need and have been looking for" individual that has been in your make-believe dream. That is standard. That is life.

The similarity would be like typing up a resume to present to a hopeful employer. Your resume presents a person who is obviously without a doubt qualified for the position. Your resume presents a person, who if you don't meet all the required qualifications for the job, is sure to be able to learn, retain, and achieve all expected tasks and duties as an employee without ever failing. Your resume presents a person who is a strongly motivated team player who understands how to work with difference people and can communicate well with others, no matter what the situation is. In addition, during the interview, you attempted to present yourself to be what you have explained yourself to be on the resume. In that interview, you attempt to be the most unique individual that has ever stepped up to the plate for the job. However, a smart employer understands that the person who shows up for the interview isn't going to be the 100 percent exact same person that shows up for work Monday morning. That's just the reality of meeting people. You get to learn their flaws over time.

I understand that situations can happen when you meet a person, and that person may completely amaze you with his or her presentation. You know that he or she must be the angel that you have been praying for. It's easy to get caught up in that first-impression person. But the flaw is when you take that first impression and allow that to be your permanent telescope in viewing that person. No matter what the person says, you only see that first impression. No matter what he or she does, you only see that first impression. When you talk about that person to your friends, you talk about the first impression person, even a year after you have been with this person already. When you meet other people, you compare them to the first impression version of your mate because you fail to see the mistakes he or she has made since you have been together. You fail to see the hints that they have been laid out for you of things they really enjoy doing and really desire. YOU FELL IN LOVE

WITH THE FIRST IMPRESSION VERSION OF YOUR MATE. You never, ever left the first date. To top it all off, your mate realizes what part of them you fell in love with and is constantly trying to fill those shoes of that first impression date. That first few weeks, it seems as if he was playing a role in an Oscar award-winning movie. And for him, the Oscar is you or worse, just your body.

He, however, becomes so infatuated with you that he attempts to assume the role of a god. He knows how you think of him. To you, he is your perfect man. To you, he will always understand you. He will never raise his voice at you. He will never mess around on you. He will not ever look at another woman and notice her attractiveness. He will always be willing to talk to you. He will always apologize first. (If there was ever anything to apologize about.) He will always open the doors for you. He will always put you first. He will always protect you. He will always call you to let you know when he is going to be late. He will always have time for you. He will always be the alibi for you to say that other girls are just jealous of what you have. He will never talk to other guys about how pretty other women look whether you are around or not. He will never want to just hang out with the guys. He will never flirt with anyone else. He will always pull the chair out for you. He will always let you walk through the door first. He will always say "I love you" around other people. He will always buy you roses for those special days. He will always help you cook and clean. He will always massage your aching muscles. He will always show respect to your family. He will always come to bed when you want him to. He will always understand when you don't want to have sex. He will always just want to hold you. He will always just want to please you, and you won't have to return the favor. He will always put you on a pedestal, and for this, you place him on a pedestal above all other guys.

In your mind, if any of these things ever change, it's not because he isn't the person you thought he was; it's because someone or something is influencing him otherwise. It's someone else's fault that he has been acting strange. You start blaming it on his friends or blaming it on his co-workers. Perhaps it's your own fault, you think. Perhaps you are the problem, you start to conclude. It never once occurred to you that … it's not simply because you didn't recognize his true identity.

Just Friends

It's a story that stands the test of time. You know, boy meets girl, girl says, "I'm only interested in being a friend," boy says, "Cool, no problem. I'm not looking for a relationship either," gets phone number, and BAM! A new potential sex partner, right? Well, not always. Most men have had that conversation or a similar conversation with a woman that they have just met. From a man's perspective, that conversation is a spark in a direction that he knows or rather thinks he may be able to score big on. All he needs is a phone number (if she gave him the correct one). The potential of him hooking up with that woman is extremely high. More than likely it will be favorable in his corner as a new sex partner or the beginning of what may develop into a non-platonic relationship. Any thoughts of the relationship growing on a "friends only" basis have never entered his mind, especially if the lady is HOT. If, by chance, the relationship becomes "friends only." That result is because of his failure, not his desire.

Now what exactly would he fail at? He would fail at not being able to seduce this woman the way he would have liked to. The cause would be that, somewhere along the lines of communication or in his acts, something transpired that he didn't do or answer correctly. But in the many days, weeks, months, and what sometimes can be years of trying, this poor fellow will never give up and likely will never give up the hopes that one day this woman will break down and want to sleep with him. He believes (like most men do) that eventually one day when this woman is lonely or is in need of some type of sympathy, counseling, or needs a shoulder to cry on that it could lead to a tunnel of ecstasy. He has heard of it being done before, and it is sure to happen to him one day (if it hasn't already happened before). All it takes is time.

Now what really has never registered in his mind is that the woman was serious when she said that she only wanted to be friends. It's common for women to want to have platonic male friends where there is nothing sexual or no intentions of an intimate relationship forming. Even in all the eating out, and movies and phone calls or even during those walks and talks, a woman can and will classify a man as being a friend and mean it in only that way. Sure, there are some women out there who say they want to be friends and don't mean it, or it's all just part of some game they may be playing just to act stuck up or appear conservative, but not every woman who says "Just Friends" is playing those games.

What he ends up doing is setting himself up for feeling used. He starts playing himself on believing a relationship is eventually going to happen. When he realizes that it's taking too long or that it isn't going to happened, he may get an attitude and throw all the things that he has done for her and all the time that he has spent with her up in the woman's face. His feelings may seem real where he may display to her that he is the victim.

He has misled himself because his relationship, from the beginning, with this woman was based on a fantasy that he refused to let go of. Every dime that he invested was an investment of hope. Every minute he spent was a sacrifice for something greater. Not to be a greater platonic friend, but to get her to trust him and depend on him. He wanted to first see what kind of man it would take to get her and what it would take for him to convince her that he was him. But it didn't matter how good-looking he was. It didn't matter how much money he had. It didn't matter how much time he spent with her because she still treated him as a friend. So he sucked it up and felt he'd blown it.

Not only did he blow it at seducing her, he, also, made himself out to be the worst. He won himself the "no sex" title. The "like a brother" title. Nevertheless, there ae some women that may still give him a chance at this level, but for most, he has no chance at the prize. The "like a brother" title is the equivalent to being nothing but a male girlfriend. To understand how all this happened, he has to go all the way back to day one. When she said "I'm not looking for a relationship but for us to be 'just friends.'" That usually translates to, "I don't find you attractive but I like your companionship." Or "you are attractive, but only enough to be an associate." See it may help to be a pretty boy to attract a woman, but it only takes communication to score. He may just lack the right communicational skills to impress that woman. And each woman is different on how he may need to approach her, and it's hard to make up for a bad approach.

For the more knowledgeable man, the best tools for learning how to spark that approach is to Number One, observe her and, Number Two, listen to her (words and reactions). He knows to pay close attention to what she is saying. With good listening skills, no matter how he looks, he feels he can attract some of the most beautiful women out there. Add a touch of humor with that, and he will definitely feel like THE MAN. He feels many women can't resist a smart, confident, and humorous man; however, even if he thinks he has those things, it still will not always guarantee that she will not give him the "like a brother" or "just friends" title eventually.

Ladies, unfortunately the way you act when you actually get a man in this stage is very close to the way you should act when you are trying to attract the man of your dreams. Keeping that wall up and turning him into a friend first gains you some major respect points from a man's point of view. That's why that male friend you have who once chased you has never stopped liking you. And you know he likes you. He can't stop liking you because you kept being a respectable woman to him. He would have been like "all the rest" if you did your normal routine of letting him take control of you or that relationship "too" soon. Usually the man that ends up being your long-term friend would make a very good mate. Well … sometimes! There are times when you feel that you know too much about a man and he knows to much about you to where you would never be able to trust one another. It is those times where it is actually best to remain just friends. When meeting a man for the first time, and you find you have an attraction to him, your training of that man begins that day. It's in that moment when, although you know you want to be more than friends, your character should portray that you want to be "just friends."

Comfortdiction

IN AN EFFORT TO SHED some light on how many men think about the really attractive tight-fitting outfit a woman may have on, I've added this for your reading pleasure. The lady says that she doesn't wear that outfit just for attention, but men end up coming on too strong, or she gets those howls and gawks as heard and seen from the stereotyped construction worker guys as she walks down the street. She feels disrespected or annoyed when they ask for her name or number, and when asked about what she has on, she says, "It's not for attention; it's because it's comfortable." She asks with an attitude why he keeps gawking at her chest and points out where her eyes are located on her head, even though her cleavage may show more than what her bra could actually hold. This is the contradiction to the comfortable reasoning she's been holding on so dear to.

This isn't training, but an explanation as to why many men are confused when they come onto a woman simply because of what she has on, and he actually does come on very strong. Sometimes his approach is dictated by your appearance and his state of mind. Here is that man's perspective.

She says it's because it's comfortable. She says, just because she has it on, that it has nothing to do with her wanting to show anything off. Even though the order for "heavily starched" was placed at the cleaners with a maximum crease, what were once loose jeans are now a pair of denim cardboard peal offs. The crease that was so wonderfully laid is only an embossed line that molds against her leg like a divider. If, by chance, there is not any starch, perhaps it was the size of the jeans themselves. She, being a size 10, buys that size 8. She does a pulling dance while putting them on which looks like a self-played game of tug of war.

She is limited in her movements because she wants to ensure that the material is securely in place as it was when she last saw it in her two-hour mirror show she performed in the bathroom. She becomes her own photographer and fills up her phone with images of butts, boobs, and kissy faces. Although she constantly believes she is overweight, the hiphuggers are accepted as the apparel of choice for the day, displaying the "I need to lose" and the "you can't really tell" at the same time. After all, she decided that she only has to suck her stomach in a little, while also reminding herself to keep her shoulders back and chest out. Piece of cake. It's comfortable.

She's finally out of the stables and heads out to the finish line or whatever destination that has called for such "comfort" and "time" to prepare for. It doesn't even take a minute before she is instantly picked up on radar from undercover eyes of prey as she walks into the establishment. She notices that many are smiling and waving at her, and she passes it off as "the people are just so nice and friendly." Not taking the time to look around to find that the smiles are now gawks from the friendly unavailable males that are mixed in the crowd. She easily finds offense when some unknown guy whistles or shouts, "DAMN! You look fine as hell in those jeans." Instinctively, she rolls her eyes and mumbles to herself, "Damn pervert" or some kind of derogatory statement. His opening statement further motivates the courage of another onlooker to immediately grab her hand and whisper to her, "Hey, baby. Let me get your number," or some other line that completely annoys her. After all, she thinks, I did not walk in displaying a sign that said, "ALL HORNY

DOGS PLEASE COME TALK TO ME."

She finally sees glimpses of familiar faces within the crowd ahead of her, and her head begins to bob like a fishing cork in floating water. Her girlfriends see her, and they greet each other with smiles, while their eyes check the other's outfit and hair out. Like her, they also have been giving their own two-hour bathroom mirror show performance. They, too, have mentally prepared themselves for the posture they must retain in order to ensure that their clothing is kept neatly in place. Some have taped their cloths onto their skin to show only 40 percent of their breasts. Some have placed napkins over their legs when they sit so as not to reveal the shadow of thigh that is only one inch from displaying their underwear. Some are constantly fighting the gravity and wind that seem to even want to undress them by forcing open the high split skirt or rolling down the latex halter top. Others have gone to war with needles and safety pins and show slight battle scars on their clothing that left marks and stretches like that of Frankenstein's skin.

Each is on guard to defend herself against anyone who dares to accuse them of dressing the way they are for the sole purpose of getting attention. The outfits they chose where chosen because they were cute, not because they wanted to show or reveal some parts of their body that would tease the average man to in-vision them nude underneath, not to taunt him into wanting to rip their clothes off immediately and lick, rub, suck, and dive into her until he explodes like a sonic boom. She isn't trying to show her stuff off like some slut on the corner trying to make a sale. She is not trying to be mistaken for a high-class call girl like those who may be spotted in Las Vegas. She isn't trying to show any percentage of hoochiness that is far from within her character. Those tight, stomach sucking, chest out, shoulders up, high heeled, short steps, covered legs, hold split, taped shirts, no bends, constant pull 'em downs, are "so comfortable."

Many men will argue that this particular type of woman, who continues to claim the comfortable alibi as to her provocative dressing, is definitely trying to get attention, even though she may oftentimes be getting the wrong attention. For, at home, her outfits consist of loose shirts from his collection that are usually twice her size. The pants are baggy jeans with maybe a hole or two, worn from the many years of wear and tear. Or maybe they are old walking shorts, or faded oversized gym shorts from high school or college that may have old bleach stains on them. Whatever the case, they are labeled as a collection of items that cannot be thrown away because "they are so damned comfortable."

www.ingramcontent.com/pod-product-compliance
Lightning Source LLC
Chambersburg PA
CBHW060340080526
44584CB00013B/846